Victorian England

Pentonville by sunset *(overleaf)*
The background is dominated by the towers and spires of the Midland
Grand Hotel at St Pancras Station, the Midland Railway's London
terminus. The station came into use on 1st October 1868 but the hotel,
designed by George Gilbert Scott, not until 5th May 1873. In front and
to the right of the huge St Pancras building is the Great Northern
Railway's rival terminus at King's Cross, by L. Cubitt, 1852

DAILY NEWS
Largest Circulation in the World

O. DAVEY & Co
BILL POSTERS
80 HIGH ST
ISLINGTON

DAILY NEWS

O. DAVEY & CO
DAILY NEWS

B. T. Batsford Ltd   London
G. P. Putnam's Sons   New York

Victorian England

W. J. Reader

Contents

© W. J. Reader, 1964, 1973
ISBN (GREAT BRITAIN) 0 7134 1441 3
Library of Congress Catalog Card Number: 73–88595
SBN (UNITED STATES) 399–11279–0
First published in this edition 1974

Phototypeset by Filmtype Services Limited, Scarborough, Yorkshire
and printed in Great Britain by
William Clowes and Sons Ltd, London and Beccles, for the publishers
B. T. Batsford Ltd, 4 Fitzhardinge Street, London W1H 0AH
G. P. Putnam's Sons, 200 Madison Avenue, New York, NY 10016

The Illustrations

Acknowledgment

For any merit this book may have, much of the credit ought to go to those who have taught me history over the last forty years or so, especially Mr J. F. Elam, formerly of Taunton School, and Professor C. H. Wilson whose pupil I still am. I should like to thank Professor Harold Perkin for the original suggestion of writing the book, and those who read and commented on the original draft: Professor Wilson and Messrs B. F. Spiller, B. Fishel and W. Meek. Mrs Meek read the book at many stages and I hope it bears some trace of her lively and penetrating mind. My wife's mother, Mrs W. V. C. Maffett, is an incomparably assiduous proof-reader. My wife herself had to endure the side effects of spare-time writing, and without her forbearance and active help the book would never have been written at all.

The illustration on page 88 appears by gracious permission of Her Majesty the Queen.

The author and publishers also wish to thank the following for the illustrations appearing in this book: The Baptist Union of Great Britain for the illustration appearing on page 173; Messrs M. Bernard for page 77; Birmingham City Museum and Art Gallery for page 53; Lord Cromer for page 30; the Trustees of the British Museum for page 204; W. & D. Downey for page 198; Glasgow Museum and Art Galleries for page 145; the Institution of Civil Engineers for page 15; Keystone for page 196; Mrs P. H. Lee-Steere for page 194; the London Museum for the illustration appearing on the title page and pages 12 and 128; the Mansell Collection for pages 24, 83, 85, 95, 108, 110, 111, 112, 114, 115, 116, 118, 120, 123, 124, 141, 159, 161, 162, 166, 186 and 190; the *Radio Times* Hulton Picture Library for pages 19, 133, 154 and 210; the Master and Fellows of St John's College, Cambridge for page 21; the Trustees of the Tate Gallery for page 61 and 148; the Directors of the Tate Gallery and the London Museum for page 92; the Victoria and Albert Museum for page 14 and the Wellcome Trustees for page 106.

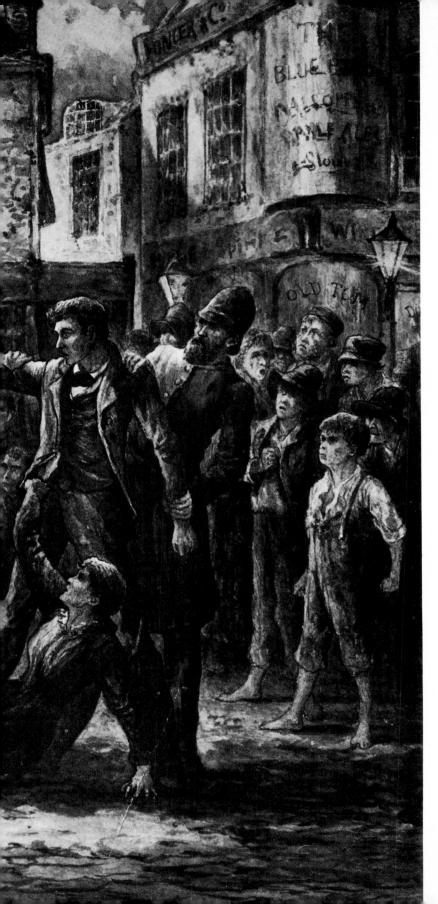

1 The Victorian setting

Middle-class comfort, as depicted in Joseph Dyckmans, 1897
'Sweetness is to woman what sugar is to fruit. It is her first business to
be happy—a sunbeam in the house, making others happy. True, she
will often have a tear in her eye, but, like the bride of young
Lochinvar, it must be accompanied with "a smile on her lips".'
Rev E. J. Hardy, Chaplain to H.M. Forces, *Manners Makyth Man,* 1887

Conference of Engineers at the Britannia Bridge, by John Lucas: Robert Stephenson is sitting in the centre, I. K. Brunel on the extreme right

There were twice as many people living in England and Wales when Queen Victoria died as there had been fifty years before. If Malthus had been right most of them should have been starving. If Marx had been right they should nearly all have been on the verge of revolution. In fact many were underfed, many were discontented, but few wished to overthrow Queen and constitution, for as a whole the English people in 1901 were better off than ever before, and they had a greater faith in peaceful reform than in violence. For they had already survived the social strain of altering, in a couple of generations, the whole basis of national life from farming to industry, from country to town. By their own efforts the Victorians had made their means of livelihood more than keep pace with their rising numbers: a thing which no one before their time would have imagined possible. And they had set an example to the world in doing it.

What kind of people were they?

Robert Stephenson's tubular Britannia Bridge over the Menai Straits under construction 1849. The railway runs through 'two independent continuous tubular beams, each 1,511 feet in length, and each weighing 4,680 tons', supported on masonry at each end and carried by three towers over the water. The tubes were floated on pontoons in sections and hoisted into position from water-level. Bridge opened 18th March 1850; cost of the whole work: £234,450

About 1840 a Lancashire cotton-printer called Thomson, accustomed to travel a good deal on business, was speaking of the qualities of the sort of men he employed. He remarked on 'the superior persevering energy of the English workman, whose untiring, savage industry surpasses that of every other country I have visited, Belgium, Germany and Switzerland not excepted'. And indeed no such explosion of human energy had ever been seen as that which was transforming England as Thomson spoke. Energy was the key quality of the Victorians—especially the early Victorians—and their characteristic achievement was the building of the railways. There were no railways at all in the modern sense before 1825. Large-scale building, encouraged by the success of the Liverpool and Manchester line, began in the thirties, getting well under way about the middle of the decade. By 1848 some 5,000 miles had been built.

These 5,000 miles, with their cuttings, embankments, tunnels, bridges and viaducts, included some of the most massive engineering works ever undertaken, and considered as a whole they were a feat of construction never previously equalled nor, perhaps, since surpassed. Engineering skill and daring, mechanical ingenuity, industrial organization—all far more advanced in England than anywhere else—all these brought the railways into being, but above everything they are the navvy's monument: the monument of that 'untiring, savage industry' which Thomson spoke of. Rock could be blasted, but there was little earth-moving machinery except primitive contraptions of ropes, horses and carts, wheelbarrows and inclined planes, and it is scarcely an exaggeration to say that the railways of England were made with pick and shovel. Moreover, the work on the earlier lines was much greater than on lines built later because the first locomotives could tackle nothing but the gentlest of slopes, so that cuttings and embankments had to be enormous to flatten out the road.

The labourers who built these works became famous throughout Europe. William Lindley, building a railway from Berlin to Hamburg in the early forties, paid English navvies 5s. (25p) a day—twice the rate for Germans. In France, too, navvies on the line between Le Havre and Paris made up in productivity what they cost in high wages. 'The most eminent employers ...', Lindley said, 'agree that it is strength of body, combined with strength of will, that gives steadiness and value to the artisan and common English labourer.' In less than twenty years, by strength of body and strength of will, the essential physical structure of Victorian England—the railway system—was planted on the landscape. Great earthworks are among the most enduring of the works of man; in two or three thousand years' time the relics of those twenty years will still be there to show where once the trains went by.

The railways were an achievement on an heroic scale, but then Queen Victoria's early years were an heroic age. This the Queen's subjects were well aware of—so much so that by 1850 they had already borrowed their sovereign's name and called themselves Victorians: a gesture which not even the subjects of Elizabeth I, in many ways so similar, had thought of. The Victorians not only built the railways but they built the towns with the same urgent energy and then, appalled

A railway navvy of about 1850, as portrayed by *Punch*, showing his usual equipment—lantern (for tunnel work), pick, shovel and wheelbarrow. The navvy's uniform consisted of heavy-duty clothes, often including white corduroy trousers and a gay handkerchief; off-duty navvies were dressed flamboyantly

at the problems which the new industrial society was creating, they investigated, criticized and reformed the condition of the people and the institutions of the State as no one before had ever dreamt of doing.

The onrush of change was in a fair way to bursting the framework of society. The machinery of government and administration which the eighteenth century had bequeathed was quite inadequate to hold things together. Facts, to start with, were almost entirely lacking; those who governed did not know what the needs of the governed were. Then the whole temper of the eighteenth century— and of the political economists who so greatly influenced early Victorian policy—was against interfering with the liberty of the governing classes: a noble ideal, no doubt, when directed against the arbitrary power of the Crown, but less admirable when it stopped Parliament from forcing corporations to make the towns hygienic or from regulating conditions of employment. The first thing Victorian reformers had to do, therefore, was to find out what had to be done. Hence the Royal Commissions, the Select Committees, the reports, returns and statistical tables, the Blue Books and White Papers which became a necessary part of the law-making process. Then, against stout individualist opposition, they had to push out the frontiers of State action so that there was a constant much-resented invasion of private right on behalf of public good and a steady build-up of the power and machinery of the central government.

Some of this activity was the result of sheer necessity, as when cholera frightened people into accepting strong measures to look after the health of towns. Some of it was the result of the interplay of party politics, as when country gentlemen saw fit to support the cause of factory legislation. A great deal of it arose from change in the balance of political power as the middle classes first and then the working classes came to the vote. But there remains much which must be put down to an awakening of the social conscience formerly unparalleled. When the Victorians are accused of self-interest it is proper to recall that the reason why we know so much about what was wrong with Victorian society is that so many people, for no selfish motive, felt a duty to put it right.

Victorian energy far overflowed the shores of England. Those who could find no fulfilment at home exported themselves all over the world, especially to the United States and the Colonies. As the Census Report of 1851 put it, emigration since 1750 had been 'to such an extent, as to

Stockport in 1850. The population of Stockport, 14,830 in 1801, was 53,835 in 1851, 92,832 by the end of the century (1901)

people large states in America, and to give permanent possessors and cultivators to the land of large colonies in all the temperate regions of the world, where . . . the people of new nations maintain an indissoluble union with the parent country'. And as well as peacefully emigrating, the Victorians embattled brought more territory under British rule—briefly, as it turned out, but enduringly, as they thought—than any other race of conquerors in history. The rule which they imposed was nearly everywhere a great improvement on what had gone before, and it has yet to be shown that what has followed it is everywhere more desirable.

The making of Victorian England was carried through in

a general spirit of self-confidence, hope and belief in the future, which at its worst might degenerate into smugness but at its best refused to regard any problem as insoluble. 'It is not for us', wrote the authors of the 1871 Census Report, 'to tell how this Empire subsists or has been built up. Yet the Census will show its essential parts in their relations to each other, constituted not only for continuance but for growth. For it is growing, increasing and multiplying still . . . the evolution of such a nation is not the result of chance; and although it cannot be traced to the policy or genius of one man it will be found to be the result of an elaborate and skilful organization acting under constant forces regulated by wiser, diviner laws than Plato gave his commonwealth.'

Energy, hope, self-confidence—all these are attributes of youth, and early Victorian England was predominantly young. This was partly because so many children were growing up and partly because, in the raw horrors of the new towns and amid the unregulated hazards of industry, many people died before they were old. The Census authorities of 1851 calculated, admittedly on shaky grounds, since many people did not know their age, that almost half the population were under twenty. At the 1871 Census the mean age was put at 26·4, and the Report comments: 'The people of England, which calls herself Old, are younger than the people of many other countries, and certainly younger than the people of the countries of stagnation.'

What also gave certainty and drive to the Victorians' manifold activities was the backing of rigid notions about the right ordering of society and individual behaviour. Later generations have pointed out the repressive effect of some of these notions and how heavily they bore down on people who defied them. In this point of view there is a good deal of truth, as some Victorians, George Eliot and Samuel Butler amongst them, were well aware.

What is often overlooked, however, is that the weight of the Victorian conscience was not universally repressive. Some very talented people found it so, and later opinion has queried the justice and the humanity of the attitude of mind which ruined Wilde, Parnell and Dilke. But the fact that unquestionable standards of right and wrong were generally held to exist, backed by the force of established authority, was an immense support to many people. They were relieved of any necessity to dissipate effort in thinking these matters out for themselves, and they could build their lives on what they believed to be unshakable foundations, going about

20

their own and their nation's work with a strength of purpose which has increasingly eluded later generations.

Moral standards, as the expressed will of God, could not be flouted without grave impiety: a point of view which emphasizes the element of authoritarianism in the Victorian outlook. From God downwards through the Queen and the established social order, there were those, it was generally held, whose place it was to give orders and those whose duty it was to obey. Obedience was one of the first of many duties exacted of a child by parents, and it was a virtue highly prized throughout society by those who considered they had a right to demand it. The political system, though it permitted a degree of personal liberty much greater than at the present day, was at the same time deeply permeated with the authoritarian idea, especially the principle that social standing carried authority with it, which was in the main long accepted by the working classes themselves, even after the Second Reform Act had created household suffrage. As late as the eighties 'democracy' was a dirty word in the political vocabulary of the ruling classes, and Escott was

Family prayers. 'Sunday 9th October 1864 . . . This evening at nine we had prayers in the library as usual; my father sitting at the centre table and reading for the twentieth time one of those good sincere old sermons, full of the simple Calvinistic Protestantism of thirty years ago.' (From the Diary of A. J. Munby, 1828–1910, quoted in *Munby, Man of two Worlds* by Derek L. Hudson, London 1972. Painting by Samuel Butler, 1864)

Paterfamilias, from an engraving
after John Leech, 1847. Evidently
time for children to go to bed

writing of 'the dream . . . of our English workmen of sending
to Parliament a number of representatives who shall form a
Labour party'.

'Authority', except in the special case of the Queen, nearly
always meant male authority. The Victorians, pious as they
were, found St Paul's text about the man being the head of
the woman exceedingly convenient and made great use of
it, as they did of the equally serviceable, 'Children, obey
your parents in the Lord.' The Queen herself, jealous though
she was of her constitutional status as Sovereign, would
hardly have quarrelled with the Baptist preacher Spurgeon
in his description of the proper relationship of man and wife
in a purely domestic setting. 'He', said Spurgeon, referring
to the husband, 'has many objects in life which she does not
quite understand; but she believes in them all, and anything
which she can do to promote them, she delights to perform.'
Even as late as the eighties, when the movement for women's

rights had made some headway, Escott still held that 'it cannot be asserted that the average woman is at any period of her life a free agent in the sense that a man is a free agent'.

The idea that women were naturally subservient to men would not have surprised the Victorians' ancestors, nor the notion that they were weaker in body and mind and generally in most ways inferior. What earlier ages would have found surprising was the Victorian insistence that women, because they were weaker, should be protected rather than exploited and also that, however inconsiderable their intellectual powers might be, they nevertheless had a purity and spirituality of mind which should be shielded from male coarseness. Some such notions as these had been part of the medieval ideal of 'chivalrous' conduct towards ladies, but that had been a courtly game, an aristocratic conceit, hardly a serious prescription for everyday life. Now the Victorians turned their own interpretation of it into one of the leading requirements of gentlemanly behaviour, backed by the same formidable sanctions which they applied to the rest of their moral code. By doing so, as in so much else that they did, they took a long stride in the direction of civilized and humane behaviour.

With their acceptance of established authority the Victorians combined a settled belief in individual responsibility and individual rights. The first followed from their ideas on morality; each man would answer for his actions, good or bad, gaining praise or blame as the case might be, and there was little disposition to admit that anyone might be undeservedly fortunate on the one hand or the victim of circumstances on the other. And with responsibility went rights: the right, principally, to pursue one's private interests according to the dictates of one's own conscience. The State, according to this view of affairs, should intervene as little as possible, and as late as the eighties it was possible to refer to the Education Act of 1870 in these terms: 'No such organized intervention between parent and child, no such systematic inquisition into those private affairs which Englishmen are in the habit of keeping religiously to themselves, had ever been attempted in this country.' And even later Charles Booth, with all his knowledge of the appalling handicaps against which the poor had to struggle, could say: 'Looked at from the side of industry, life presents itself as full of chances, the best use of which demands free individuality. . . . The chances that offer, to be grasped or missed with reward or penalty attached, make of men's lives

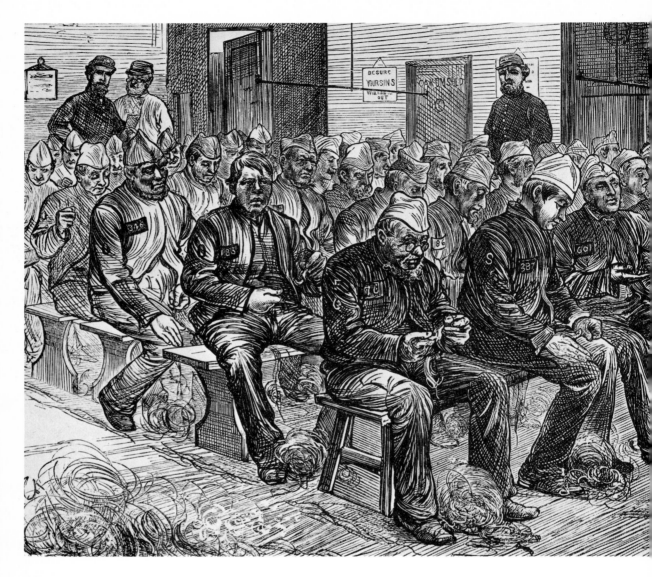

House of Correction in
Clerkenwell, which could
accommodate up to 2,000
prisoners. 'The work of picking
oakum is rather painful to
delicate fingers, but becomes easy
after a few days . . . The prisoners
. . . are forbidden to speak a word
to each other when assembled for
work or dinner; even a detected
glance or sign can be severely
punished. Each person is locked
up at night in a solitary cell.'
(*The Illustrated London News*,
17th January 1874)

a struggle which never ends and which falls very hardly on
some; but from this very struggle the whole community, and
every individual in it, undoubtedly gains.'

From individual enterprise, as Booth observed, everyone
seemed to have gained; that, at any rate, was a central tenet
of middle-class orthodoxy. And the sixty years of Queen
Victoria's reign were above all the sixty years of the middle-
class man. As he watched the nation's prosperity rising with
his own he saw no reason to doubt that this happy process
flowed from the exercise of the middle-class virtues of
sobriety, thrift, piety and hard work. As he came to the

central positions of power in the State he did his best to convert the rest of the nation to his own way of thinking.

In the life of Georgian and Regency England—which in many ways can hardly be said to have ended much before the repeal of the Corn Laws—the middle-class Victorian saw little to admire and much to reconstruct. For its material relics, particularly its architecture, he had no use at all. 'In the first quarter of the eighteenth century,' wrote H. D. Traill in the nineties, 'architecture, as a living art, had been laid to rest in the grave of Wren.' As for the ramshackle structure of public administration, it was investigated and briskly toned up, partly by the application of that infallible test of merit both academic and moral, the written examination. As Benjamin Jowett, Fellow and Tutor of Balliol, wrote to Sir Charles Trevelyan in 1854: 'for the moral character of the candidates I should trust partly to the examination itself. . . . The perseverance and self-discipline necessary for the acquirement of any considerable amount of knowledge are a great security that a young man has not led a dissolute life.'

'Dissolute life' was pretty generally regarded as characteristic of eighteenth-century behaviour, and a powerful movement against it had been gathering force since Wesley's time. Before we sneer at the exaggerated primness of the Methodists and their allies it is well to recall that many eighteenth-century ways, behind the elegant façade of upper-class courtesy and taste, were not pretty at all. There was great brutality and great coarseness, both of which the Victorians did a good deal to remove from English life. Moreover, again following paths first marked out in the late eighteenth century itself, they carried on the process of cleaning up public life. Corruption at parliamentary elections, it is true, went on until vote by ballot and an immensely enlarged electorate put an end to it, and corruption in one form or another is hardly likely ever to disappear entirely; but if it has become the shameful exception rather than the tolerated rule, then that is something more which can be laid to the credit of Victorian ideas of moral rectitude.

The end of the eighteenth-century social order on the Continent, with its aristocratic polish, its free thought and its godlessness, had been bloody revolution, twenty years' war and then a series of other revolutions, in France and elsewhere, during the first half of the nineteenth century. And what had happened elsewhere might happen here, or at any rate most reasonably well-off Englishmen, up to about

The custodian of middle-class morality, from an engraving after Thomas Seccombe, c.1877

1850, thought so; and as long as any considerable number of Chartists believed in 'physical force' rather than 'moral force' they may have been right. They could point to the rioting and bloodshed in Newport and in Bristol in the thirties. They could quote, as Engels did, from speeches such as the one made by Stephens, a Methodist minister, in 1838, in which he said to Manchester working men '... you have a weapon ... against which bayonets and cannon are powerless, and a child of ten years can wield it. You have only to take a couple of matches and a bundle of straw dipped in pitch, and I will see what the Government and its hundreds of thousands of soldiers will do against this one weapon if it is used boldly.' And indeed it was used in the countryside during the distress of the thirties and forties, when unpopular farmers' flaming ricks were no very uncommon sight. After about the middle of the century the danger of revolution rapidly dwindled, though even in the mid-eighties the idea of a working-class rising could still be seriously discussed in print.

26

Quite apart from the risk of revolution, violence was never very far under the surface, though much better controlled than formerly. The police had been invented about eight years before the Queen's accession. They were not, at first, regarded with much favour even by the law-abiding, who saw in them, as their ancestors had seen in the standing army, a threat to civil liberties. But as the years went on they brought the turbulence of cities under restraint, and the views of the respectable changed. 'In the new, raw, crude, growing town', as G. E. Diggle says of Widnes, 'deeds of violence were . . . all too frequent'; and property needed protection, too. Quite soon prosperous citizens began to look on the police in the same light as their own trusted upper servants. Notices went up like the one in Lincoln's Inn: 'The Porters and Police have orders to remove all Persons making a noise within this Inn.'

The law, less savage than in the eighteenth century, still met violence with brutality. Transportation went on until 1846. The prison system was explicitly punitive; rehabilitation had little part. Public hangings, until 1868, were a spectacle of immense popularity. Overnight huge crowds would pack the streets outside the gaol, singing, drinking, fighting. Every householder remotely within sight of the scaffold could expect to pack his windows with paying customers.

Strikes were generally expected to be violent, sometimes to the extent of needing troops to control them. Two miners were shot dead near Pontefract in 1893 by soldiers acting in

NOTICE!!!

The MINERS of the Dudley District are respectfully informed

THAT

A Public Meeting

Will be held at *The 5 Ways* on *Monday Oct 7*

On business of importance to their welfare, and for the purpose of petitioning the next Sessions of Parliament to pass an **Eight Hours' Bill** for the Regulating and Working the Mines and Collieries of Great Britain.

The Meeting will be addressed by Mr. WM. DANIELLS, Editor of the *Miners' Advocate*, and one of the Agents of the MINERS' NATIONAL ASSOCIATION; also, by other friends of the Rights of Labour. Chair taken at *Three* o'clock.

Miners Attend, Remember "UNION IS STRENGTH."

(GOODWIN, PRINTER, NEW-ST., DUDLEY.)

A miners' meeting—early Victorian poster

aid of the civil power. Trade unions sometimes organized campaigns of terrorism. For ten years or more during the late fifties and early sixties small unions in the building trades near Manchester plagued employers—themselves not much better off than the unionists and sometimes related to them—with beatings, incendiarism, bombing and the destruction of livestock and property. The causes of quarrel were the employment of non-unionists, the use of machinery and the use of bricks made in one union's territory in the territory of another. The outrages were discussed and authorized at union meetings, and some men did very well out of perpetrating them. They were shipped to America at the unions' expense if pursuit got too hot, or defended if they were caught. The cost, which ran into thousands, was all met from union funds and duly audited.

For the first dozen years or so of Queen Victoria's reign, then, there was a lively fear or hope of revolution, depend-

Outside the Cou
before a public h
Punch, 1849. Be
1830, of 408 mer
London of capi
were hanged;

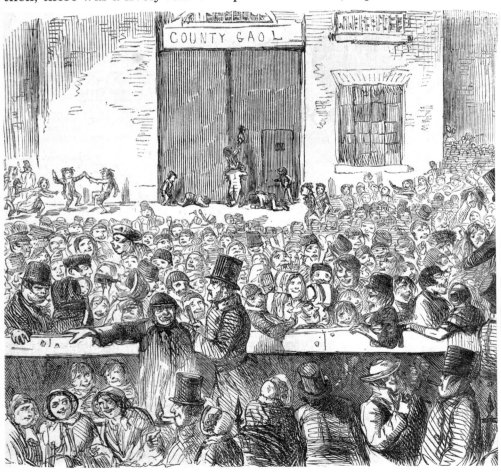

in ___ side of the barricades you expected to be. Even wh ___ at died away, the ordinary and ancient violence of town life, so much more threatening now that towns were so much bigger, was barely being brought under control. Strikes were always likely to be stormy. It was not hard to stir up mobs at elections, at political meetings, and generally in times of national excitement, as when the Austrian general Haynau was attacked by brewers' draymen in 1849 because they believed he had been responsible for brutality to women in repressing the Hungarian rising of 1848. As late as 1886 the windows of clubs in Pall Mall were broken by rioters. It is not surprising that the ordinary Victorian of the comfortable classes, contemplating all this violence from his own quiet fireside and recalling what elderly people told him about even worse disturbances within their memory, placed respectability, orderly behaviour and due deference to established authority high in his scale of values.

The early Victorians built their England on the confidence that came of having beaten the great Napoleon, and in their dealings with the outside world they made it plain that they were quite prepared to do the same sort of thing again if need be. They were not aggressive—they had no need to be—but they had no great dread of war, and their national totem was more like the truculent, swaggering John Bull of the eighteenth century than the subdued conciliator of later times. And they showed the same sturdy nationalism in the name they applied to their country. Nearly always, even on Scotch or Irish lips, it was 'England', as it still is to most foreigners, and very rarely 'Great Britain' or 'the United Kingdom', those accurate but cumbersome portmanteaux.

The young Queen's England led the world, and her subjects knew it. They were building the first great industrial power, which foreigners regarded with the mixture of awe and envy later transferred to the United States of America. The whole basis of English life was changing, and changing much faster than in any of the other social upheavals which England, in her long history, had undergone. The ancient social order of the countryside, with its roots running back into prehistory, was giving place to a strange new town-based society of machinery and mass production, looking to the twentieth century and beyond.

That is the theme of this book.

(Overleaf) The hunt breakfast, from a painting by Sir Francis Grant, 1834. The breakfast is at Melton. The artist, a Scotsman, was intended for the law but, according to Sir Walter Scott, 'was passionately fond of fox-hunting and other sports . . . . He had also a strong passion for painting', from which he made his career

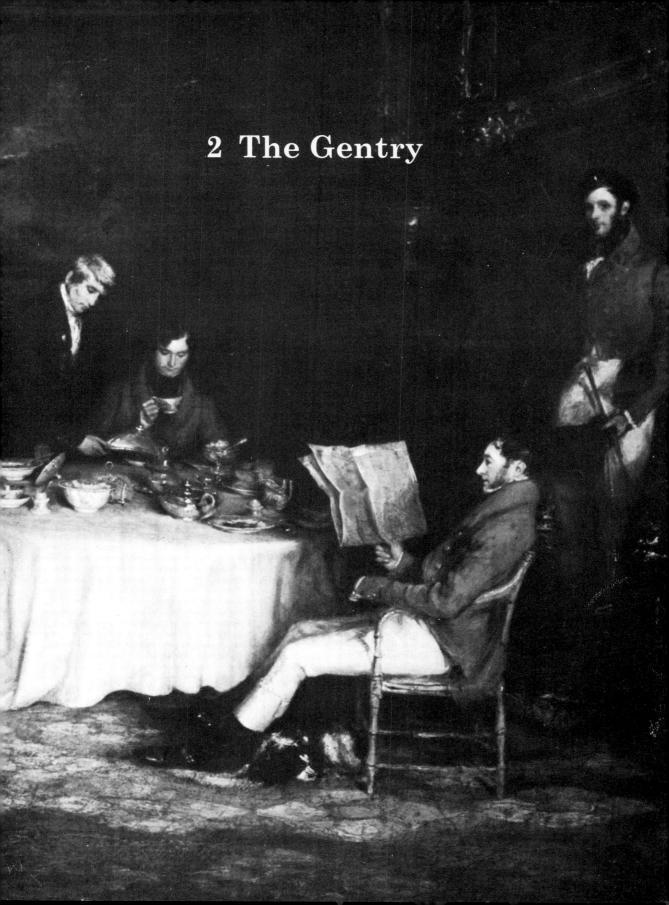

2 The Gentry

A novelist of 1897 is introducing her central characters: 'Just below and before them rose an ancient gateway, iron and stone, with much heraldic ornament. An ivy-mantled lodge with curly chimney-stacks stood immediately within; and beyond, sloping gently upward for a mile or more, a straight, grassed, drive between thick woods—a beautiful green vista, three times as wide as an ordinary park avenue —was closed, on an elevated horizon, by the indistinct but imposing mass of a great grey house, one of those "stately homes of England" which are our pride and boast.'

England in 1897 had been thoroughly industrialized for many years. Most people's livelihood, the greater part of the national wealth and the country's international standing depended more or less directly on mines, factories and world-wide trade. The 'landed interest' had so far lost control of affairs that most of the nation's food came in, untaxed, from abroad, making great difficulties for the farmer and his landlord. Nevertheless, the squires' prestige remained immense. In the year of the Diamond Jubilee, Keir Hardie's cloth cap had already been seen in Parliament, but not many people would have quarrelled with the idea that the gentry and the 'stately homes' which symbolized their way of life were England's 'pride and boast'.

The respect which people had for the gentry was one source of their strength. Even more important was their property. The two between them gave independence, the gentleman's leading characteristic. The landowner with a sufficient estate was beholden to no one for his social position or for his wealth; both were his by right. Within the limits of the law, his income and his own conscience, he could do pretty much as he liked. Low people might have to consider the good opinion of customers or employers; the gentleman need care for neither. The careful constraints of middle-class respectability were not for him unless he chose. His security gave him self-confidence, a good deal of arrogance, often a taste for eccentric behaviour.

The 'landed gentry' covers a wide range, from the untitled owners of comparatively small estates, wholly agricultural, up to the great ducal families—Devonshire, Bedford, Northumberland and the rest—whose immense properties included thousands of acres of farm land, large areas of London and other towns, mining rights, market rights, and so on. Between the two ends of the scale the difference was one of wealth rather than quality, and the smaller gentry were not readily disposed to admit that the great peers were

A stately country residence: Osborne House, Isle of Wight. Built 1844–48 for Queen Victoria and Prince Albert, as a private house, *not* a palace, by Thomas Cubitt the property developer. Design heavily influenced by Prince Albert

socially superior, titles notwithstanding. There was, in fact, a genuine community of interest and of outlook, because the whole system depended on the ownership of estates which passed down the generations from father to eldest son. Younger sons had to be provided for, or to provide for themselves, and daughters had to marry as judiciously as possible, so as to secure a proper position for themselves and at the same time to maintain the honour and interest of their families.

This chapter gives a sketch of the educational background of the Victorian gentry, then an indication of the traditional occupations which a gentleman might follow before he came into his estate or if, as a younger son, he had no estate to come into, and finally some account of the owners of estates themselves—the 'landed gentry' proper. But it should be borne in mind that there was no very rigid separation between the gentry and the upper end of the middle classes. Some boys of good family, without money of their own or 'expectations', went into middle-class professional pursuits (see Chapter 7), especially the law, and even into trade, as they had done in previous centuries.

The sons of the gentry had at one time commonly been educated privately or had gone to the local grammar school. By Victoria's time the grammar schools were in decay, boarding schools were becoming increasingly fashionable and easier and cheaper to reach, by rail, and private education was becoming more and more a thing for the girls only. The great development of girls' boarding schools (see Chapter 7) came in the fifties, but the upper classes did not take to them very readily. They were very much the creation of serious-minded middle-class intellectuals.

Boys' education took money for granted and treated the making of it with the contempt which only a secure income can afford. It assumed that a gentleman was by right a member of the ruling class, not to be questioned by his inferiors nor over-ready to accept superior authority: answerable only to his own notions of right and wrong. An Oxford don of the fifties, no doubt somewhat crusty, put it in this way: 'To spend more than their income, to waste their time, and to be moderately disorderly in conduct, have been and still are so usual in ordinary English education of the upper classes, that they are tolerated by a very indulgent treatment in society, treated as privileges of the rich and easy classes, and only complained of by the vast majority of such classes when they lead to too marked a failure, or to too heavy bills.'

This was a view of upper-class education which those magisterial clergymen, the reforming headmasters of early Victorian public schools, did their best to put right. In Arnold's words to his praepostors at Rugby, 'What we must look for ... is, 1st, religious and moral principles; 2ndly, gentlemanly conduct; 3rdly, intellectual ability.' His method of gaining his ends, and the method of other reformers, was to let the school run itself, under his authority, pretty much as a self-governing republic. Responsibility for discipline outside the class room and for most of the social life of the school he placed firmly in the hands of the senior boys.

This was the 'monitorial system'. It was not invented by

Victorian headmasters. It had grown up in schools so badly understaffed that the masters, acting on much the same principles as warders in an understaffed prison, had found themselves forced to rely on the good offices of the boys themselves. But the reformers took the system over, regularized it, made a virtue of it and pointed out what a good method it was for training the future rulers of England and (later) the British Empire (though in fact many Imperial administrators were Scots and Irishmen who had never been to English public schools). By the middle sixties H. M. Butler, Headmaster of Harrow, was so enthusiastic about the monitorial system that he declared 'no great school could long live in a healthy state without it'. He overlooked—or did he?—the fact that at Eton the monitorial system, if it had ever existed, had for many years been in decline.

As the monitorial system, combined with fagging, was relied on to train the character of the upper classes, so 'classical training' was the main, in fact almost the only, instrument for training the intellect. At Rugby in the sixties, seventeen out of twenty-two school hours in the

In the schoolroom, from an engraving after Charles Keene, 1882. The master wears full academical dress and is probably a clergyman. Who is the mysterious figure in the left background?

During the match, from an engraving after Arthur Hughes for Thomas Hughes' *Tom Brown's Schooldays*, 1857. Tom Brown on the bench; Arthur on the ground; a clerical schoolmaster in the background. He says: 'I'm beginning to understand the game scientifically. What a noble game it is, too!' 'Isn't it? But it's more than a game. It's an institution,' said Tom. 'Yes,' said Arthur, 'the birthright of British boys old and young, as *habeas corpus* and trial by jury are of British men.'

week were spent on the classics, in one form or another, and the curriculum at other public schools was similar. This overwhelming concentration on Latin and Greek was defended unhesitatingly by the headmasters of the nine 'great schools' which were investigated by Lord Clarendon's Commission in the sixties. After all, as several of them said, if anything else were to be taken as seriously as the classics, who would teach it, and from what books? And those who suggested that it might be a good idea to give some boys, at any rate, something like professional training were met by the thunders of Mr Gladstone, who wrote of 'the low utilitarian argument in matter of education, for giving it what is termed a practical direction', and concluded, 'I think we may on the whole be thankful that the instincts of the country have resisted what in argument it has been ill able to confute.'

How the 'low utilitarian argument' was pressed home, in spite of Mr Gladstone, is discussed in Chapter 7. Here it is sufficient to remark that the classical training was wasted on the majority of boys. It was a dull, unimaginative grind which none but the toughest intellectual constitutions could survive, let alone get any pleasure out of, and most boys left school with very little classical learning to show for seven or eight years spent in acquiring it. 'The Greek and Latin grammars, and portions of the easier classic authors—cricket—boating—the price of tarts, and of wine by the bottle, and perhaps the names of the head and assistant masters of the school; these are the particulars of their vast sum of knowledge', said a writer of 1850, dealing with public schoolboys.

But most upper-class boys were not sent to a public school to become scholars, but to become reasonably well-educated men of the world, to meet other boys of their own kind and to develop 'character'. Taking account of these parental motives, of the extreme unattractiveness, for most boys, of the subjects of formal education, and of the fact that the running of the boys' affairs was very much in their own hands, it is not surprising that outdoor activities became so important in public schools and the source of almost all prestige. Until about the seventies, team games (see Chapter 8) were not highly organized, by present-day standards, but well before that, along with other activities such as cross-country running and cadet corps, they began to loom large in school life, and in the early sixties it was estimated that a Harrow boy might spend fifteen hours a week at cricket, or twenty if he took 'every opportunity'.

If a boy went on to Oxford or Cambridge, he would find himself in an atmosphere that was partly a prolongation of public school life, partly heavily clerical. Games and rowing were important, and success in them a certain road to prestige, but the pressure to take part would not be quite so heavy as at school. On the academic side, the classics were still considered fundamental, though other subjects were thrust in as the century went on: even such things as science and engineering. Most undergraduates would aim at a pass degree or moderate success in honours, but for the academically ambitious the competition was keen, the standards were high, and there was plenty to aim at in the shape of prizes, medals and university scholarships. University teaching, like schoolmastering, was overwhelmingly in the hands of clergymen, and before 1870, while it was illegal to have a fellowship and a wife at the same time, the dons were mostly young parsons scarcely over the threshold of their careers. As to the undergraduates, in the fifties the bulk of them would be intending to take orders, but later on, under

the influence of such men as Jowett at Balliol, more conscious efforts were made at the universities to turn out civil servants, politicians and men of affairs generally. Thenceforward, with sweeping alterations in the kind of subjects that could be taken and in the method of teaching them, the universities ceased to be the closed clerical corporations that they had been formerly.

Not that life at the universities, even under clerical rule, was trammelled by any great degree of pious austerity. Royal Commissioners reporting on Oxford in 1852 drew attention to 'sensual vice, gambling . . . and extravagant expenditure', and under the last head they spoke of expensive tastes in furniture and decoration, tobacconists' bills running to £40 a year, the habit of dining at inns, taverns and clubs, and 'driving, riding and hunting'. The well-to-do young man did not go to the university, any more than he

The Oxford Commemoration, 1870. 'The upper gallery was thronged, as usual, by these young gentlemen, who amused themselves, as they always do, before the Chancellor came in, by calling for cheers or groans for different public persons, and making what noises they pleased.' (*The Illustrated London News,* 2nd July 1870)

Life at the University, from an engraving after John Leech, 1851

Prince Albert Victor of Wales,
Duke of Clarence (1864–1892),
eldest son of Albert Edward,
Prince of Wales, later King
Edward VII, went to Trinity
College, Cambridge, in 1883.
This drawing, from *Punch*, is part
of a close and rather malicious
parody of a page published in *The
Illustrated London News* a week
earlier. The Prince was not
remarkable for academic ability

had gone to school, for scholarship. He went to complete his education as a man of the world, and, as it was said of a young peer who left Oxford in 1865, 'for him and his set the University of Oxford simply did not exist. It was just Christ Church . . . and to them Christ Church meant Bullingdon, "Loder's" or "The Rousers", fox-hunting, racing, a not too serious form of cricket, and no end of good dinners in the company of the best fellows in the world as they knew it.'

An alternative to the university for a few years in the life of the heir to an estate, or a career for a younger son, was the Army. Until about the middle of the century the idea that an army officer (other than a gunner or an engineer) needed much in the way of professional education was considered eccentric and rather ungentlemanly. So also was the idea that officers should take any very close interest in the welfare of their men, an attitude perhaps reflected in the fact that in 1860 about one man in four of the Foot Guards stationed in London was said to have syphilis.

The early Victorian army officer needed money to buy his commission and a private income to live as a gentleman should (and this continued to be desirable throughout the reign), so that in general he had to be fairly well off, although even before 1870 it was possible to get a commission through Sandhurst without purchase, and R.E. and R.A. officers, who went through Woolwich, never had to purchase. It was possible for an officer to live on his pay, though he might find it hard and he might have to put up with a good deal of contempt. But the serious soldiers—those who were in the service professionally rather than socially—were inclined to come from the Irish gentry rather than the English, because the Irish were poorer and more often had to seek a living for themselves.

The Crimean War demonstrated both the strength and the weakness of the early Victorian army. Both officers and men displayed immense courage and toughness: that was taken for granted. But the administrative efficiency of Wellington's campaigns had entirely disappeared, and the general professional incompetence displayed by officers of all ranks must surely have been fatal against any other European power than Russia. When these lessons, reinforced by those of the Indian Mutiny, had been taken to heart, and when the country had seen the exploits of the Prussian army in the sixties and in 1870–71, the British army was taken in hand and all its officers (except a few from the militia) were required to undergo formal military education either at

Sandhurst or Woolwich. Even more startling to soldiers of the old school might have been Lord Wolseley's remarks in his *Soldier's Pocket Book* of 1882. 'In our intercourse with the rank and file', he wrote, '. . . let us sink as far as possible the respective titles of officers, sergeants and privates, merging them all into the one great professional cognomen of soldier. . . . The officer should take a lively interest in their amusements, encouraging them in the practice of all manly sports. In fine he should sympathize with their likes and dislikes, their pleasures and annoyances, being ready at all times to listen attentively to their grievances . . . until at last they regard him as one of themselves, a companion and a friend.'

Thus the Army, like other occupations in Victorian England, was forced into greater and greater professionalism as time went on, until even those who took commissions without any intention of soldiering for life found that they had to pay some attention to the technicalities of war and to the care of their men. The result was a very great increase in

Army Officers, from an engraving after John Leech, 1853. 'The dawdling military fop of St James's Street, when taken to the field of battle, shows not only a courage which nothing can appall, but a cool endurance amid circumstances of distraction and dismay, of which perhaps a quicker sensibility would be incapable.' W. Johnston, 1851

efficiency, in spite of the fact that in socially desirable regiments, particularly in the cavalry, it was 'not done' to go to the Staff College until well into the twentieth century. The Navy, unlike the Army, had required professional skill in its officers long before Victoria's reign, and a naval career had been a lifetime's occupation far more generally than a career in the Army. Naval officers, entering the service very young, missed much of the ordinary education of boys of their own social standing and were something of a class apart, especially since a naval career was very much a matter of family tradition, but in comparatively few families.

Alongside the armed services, the other traditional occupation for gentlemen was the Church, partly because, as with the Army and the Navy, family influence counted for a good deal in getting appointments and preferment. Also, since the organization of the Church of England was based on the needs of the old agricultural society rather than the new industrial one, it was an occupation particularly congenial to men brought up to the tastes and way of life of country gentlemen. Great religious zeal or an overpowering vocation were not generally expected—they might even be deplored—but rather a general assent to the doctrines of the Church of England and a sense of what was seemly, from the point of view of the upper classes, in village life.

In a village, the parson might well be the only educated man, or the only one apart from the squire, if there was one. He might, in fact, be the squire himself. At Lympsham, in Somerset, two rectors, father and son, saw out the whole of Victoria's reign, and they owned most of the village. Prebendary Stephenson, who was rector from 1844 to 1901, largely rebuilt the village, in a uniform neo-Gothic style, and it remains his monument. In another part of Somerset, Prebendary Thomas Sweet-Escott, rector of Brompton Ralph from 1802 to 1842, owned Hartrow Manor nearby, where he lived. He was followed in the living by a son, who held it first from 1842 to 1853 and then from 1874 to 1884, so that for over sixty years that living was in the hands of one family of local landowners.

Country parsons, though not usually zealots, were urged by the intense religious feeling of the day, High Church or Low, to press their duties a good deal more vigorously than clergymen of the eighteenth century. Parson Woodforde in George III's time—by no means unconscientious—had considered his duty done with one Sunday service a week and

holy communion three times a year. The Victorian parson, 'high' or evangelical, would hardly consider his ministry adequately performed without at least two Sunday services, fairly frequent communion, and perhaps weekday services as well. The further towards the higher reaches he went, the more services there would be, but he might have to beware of arousing suspicions of papistical practices if he went too far. Many Victorian parsons, trying to get more seemliness and dignity into churches and church ceremonies long neglected, ran into opposition over matters accepted today as traditional, such as chanting the psalms, wearing a surplice and placing the communion table as an altar at the east end of the church.

The parson might busy himself, too, with other matters which his predecessors had overlooked or neglected. The church would almost certainly need attention. It might have to be repaired or enlarged and the decoration (or lack of it) and furnishings would hardly agree with Victorian taste, especially if they dated from the previous century. Some parsons were very drastic. Prebendary J. E. Lance, rector of Buckland St Mary in Devon from 1830 to 1885, had a medieval church entirely pulled down and replaced by a very ambiti-

A country rectory, from a design by Maurice B. Adams, 1888. Of 10,478 benefices in 1836, 7,890 provided incomes between £50 and £400 a year, 297 below £50, 2,107 between £400 and £1,000, and 184 over £1,000, including 118 over £2,000. Perhaps this rector had one of those, or private means, because clerical incomes did not alter greatly during the century

ous, very Gothic structure which was consecrated in 1863. The rector of North Tuddenham in Norfolk was said to have spent more than £5,000 on the rectory, church and schools of his parish. At Snargate in Romney Marsh, the rector, Edward Wilkinson M.A., Ph.D. (an unusual degree for a Victorian clergyman), restored his church during the early seventies and is commemorated by a plaque on which he is described as 'a decided preacher of the Doctrines of God's Free and Sovereign Grace in the Salvation of his Elect', which has an austerely protestant ring about it. All over the country, in short, the revived religious zeal of Victorian England and the prosperity of the countryside were reflected in churches restored, refurnished, redecorated and sometimes entirely rebuilt.

In the parish generally the parson or his wife might see that the poor got soup in cold weather and his daughter might provide baby clothes for village mothers (recovering them after each confinement). He would oversee the village school, arriving occasionally as a figure of majesty to examine the pupils, but he would be unlikely to teach regularly there. He might be asked to draw a tooth for an old woman or to explain a legal document to an illiterate man. In his own house he might take pupils—boys who, for one reason or another, were not at a public school, or who needed coaching such as Oscar Browning had from his parson brother William before he went to Eton in 1851. He might occupy himself with works of scholarship varying from the study of local antiquities to theology. And he would very likely be a practical farmer of his glebe land.

The parson who was also a magistrate became rarer during Victoria's reign, but in all things he was a figure of authority and his parishioners were likely to hold him somewhat in awe, especially the poorer of them. Even against the squire the parson's position was very strong, and in a quarrel he might prevail. William Wayte Andrew, vicar of Ketteringham in Norfolk from 1835 to 1887, spent many years in bitter dispute with Sir John Boileau. The battle wavered, but in the end the vicar won; not least, perhaps, because his powerful preaching swayed the minds of the women at the Hall. In general it was to be hoped that squire and parson would get on together, for then the powers of Church and State, united, made for the tranquil running of local affairs.

Being a parson, like being a soldier or a sailor, was a tradition in some families. The Stephensons of Lympsham

The village parson, from an engraving after Charles Keene, 1882. This parson evidently does not think it necessary to wear distinctive 'clerical dress', which would have included a low-crowned hat and a 'dog-collar'

44

had provided parsons in Yorkshire, father and son, for well over a hundred years before they migrated to Somerset. The Sweet-Escott who was rector of Brompton Ralph from 1802 to 1842, himself the son of a clergyman, had six sons, five of whom took orders, and two of his daughters, out of three who married, had clerical husbands, one of whom was himself a member of a Somerset county family. The one layman among Sweet-Escott's sons went into Parliament and married a lady from another family of Somerset gentry.

County society, as this example shows, had a very close-knit texture. The land, the Church and Parliament, all were caught up and held together in an intricate web of family relationships which outsiders found hard to penetrate, and in the old agricultural England the landowners had commanded all the heights of profit and of power. In the new industrial England that was no longer so, but so great was the prestige of 'the County' that the new men of power, their fortunes made, sought to join it rather than overthrow it, and the facade which industrial England presented to the world, late in the nineteenth century, still had a misleadingly countrified look about it.

The squirearchy, indeed, reached the peak of its prosperity during the thirty years or so after its political influence had been overridden in the repeal of the Corn Laws. Its prosperity rested on the unprecedented demand for food from the industrial towns, of which the landed gentry were so ignorant and so scornful. Farmers could sell pretty well all they could produce, and they had very little competition from abroad. From about 1870 onwards, however, things began to change, slowly at first and then with a rush. Dutch merchants began to market a cheap substitute for butter. The Continent recovered from the wars of the sixties. Fast ocean transport and refrigerated storage enabled ranchers and farmers in Argentina, Australia and New Zealand to compete in England. Tinned meat began to come from Argentina in the sixties. In 1879 the first chilled meat came from Australia; in 1881, the first from New Zealand. Most serious of all the Americans, the Civil War over, thrust railroads into the meat and grain lands of the Far West. And all this food came in untaxed. With the import of American wheat, from the late seventies onward, the prosperity of British farming began to crumble, but no Government would dare to bring back the Corn Laws. The landowners' prop—prosperous farming—was knocked from under them, but while it was there it contributed powerfully to the feel-

The squire out shooting, from an engraving after Charles Keene, 1866. 'Rough shooting', not the elaborate ritual, just becoming popular (and *very* expensive) of employing troops of beaters to send flights of birds over lines of 'butts' where the squire and his guests would await them, instead of walking them up with dogs as this squire is doing

ing of ordered, ancient stability which mid-Victorian England so transiently enjoyed.

The nineteenth Lord Willoughby de Broke, looking back in his autobiography from the early 1920s, thought that his father, between 1850 and 1880, had enjoyed the country gentleman's golden age, when incomes were higher than they had ever been before and no one questioned the squire's social position. The period was 'untouched by the now formidable symptoms of industrialism'—an extraordinary thing to say of England in the third quarter of the nineteenth century, which shows how far out of touch a landowner could be with what was going on around him—'and the untoward manifestations of the thing called democracy'. What that meant was that the power of Quarter Sessions was not threatened—let alone overthrown—until the passing of the County Councils Act of 1888, and the squires could hunt and shoot to their hearts' content with no one to say them nay. And all the time, thanks to modern science, the breed of hunters and the make of guns was improving. No one had yet brought in high income tax or crippling estate duties, so the squires could entertain both above and below stairs 'in a manner that was the rightful heritage of the nation that had beaten the great Napoleon'. Life was quite as rich as in the time of their ancestors and a great deal more comfortable, thanks to nineteenth-century inventions, especially, in Lord Willoughby de Broke's opinion, anaesthetics.

All this represented a great deal of money. The estates of the greater peers would have a turnover running into six figures. Lord Willoughby de Broke did not profess to regard himself as more than a country gentleman, but he owned 18,000 acres and he said in his autobiography that 12,000 would bring in £12,000 to £15,000 a year. The claims on an estate would be heavy, since it was the property of a family rather than of the owner for the time being, who, as far as settled land was concerned, was no more than a life tenant. There would be portions to be found for daughters—and for younger sons—and there might be a dowager (even, sometimes, more than one) whose jointure must be paid. Nevertheless de Broke, speaking of the £12,000 to £15,000 income, considered that by the time taxes, management expenses, repairs and so on had been met there might be about £5,000 a year 'to pay for . . . hunting and entertaining'. On that 'you could almost keep a pack of fox-hounds . . . and still have something to spare'.

From this point of view, readily understandable by many,

perhaps most, country gentlemen, an estate was mainly a source of finance for hunting and entertaining. Many squires would have thought it proper to add shooting as well. Hunting, shooting and field sports generally symbolized the outdoor life which the gentry as a class regarded as the only proper life for a man. It called for many of the virtues— essentially military virtues, though practised in a civilian setting—which the gentry admired. Therefore sport acquired moral, almost mystical attributes as well as being an absorbing pastime. 'Sport' meant blood sports. Team games developed much later, with middle-class suburban associations.

Sport was expensive and it broke more than one ancient family. Moreover, there were plenty of other possibilities of extravagance to tempt the weak-minded or the eccentric, and the ruined gentleman was a fairly familiar figure. In the sixties the vicar of East Dereham in Norfolk came across 'mad Wyndham', whose sanity had been the subject of judicial enquiry. Declared sane, he had wasted his substance and, as the vicar put it, 'had degraded himself to become the driver of a stagecoach. His magnificent Felbrigg estate is

The pursuit of sport: fox-hunting, from an engraving after John Leech. The Master, presumably, and the chief of the 'hunt servants', the huntsman

sold to a mercantile man, one Kitton, so that the saying is "Windham has gone to the dogs and Felbrigg to the Kittons." Nor was Wyndham the only East Anglian coach-driver of gentle birth. Sir St Vincent Hynde Cotton of Madingley Hall near Cambridge, sixth baronet and the son of an Admiral, fell by way of high play to driving a coach on the Brighton road under the name of Sir Vincent Twist. And there were George Osbaldeston early in Victoria's reign— the 'Squire of England'—and Henry Chaplin towards its end, both of whom impaired large fortunes in the cause of sport.

The general run of squires, no doubt, were moderate, prudent men with a fairly good head for business—something which has never been lacking in the English upper class. T. H. S. Escott, himself a member of a Somerset county family, suggests that a typical squire in the seventies—'not a very great landlord'—might have rather more than £3,000 a year (presumably net income) from land. Besides that—it is the period of Trollope's *The Way We Live Now*, when city finance and the gentry were getting somewhat mixed up together—the squire might have 'judicious and profitable investments'. He could be in Parliament (and if he stood locally he would certainly expect his tenants' votes to help get him there). He could keep his labourers' cottages in proper repair. He could give largely to local funds and build 'very handsome schools' but 'he has never been guilty of the indiscriminate bounty which is the parent of pauperism'. His affairs would be managed by an agent, 'a respectable gentleman, who has no social ambition of an aggressive character'. Another squire might look after his property himself, except when he needed expert advice, and then, in Escott's view, he would have 'as few spare moments as a city clerk'.

A country gentleman might live virtually his whole life, once he came to his estate, within the borders, social and geographical, of 'the County'. Unless he was a very great landowner indeed he would be unlikely to own a house in London, though he might take one for 'the season' when his daughters were marriageable or for the session if he was in Parliament. He would have seen the world as a young man— in the Army, perhaps, or in the diplomatic service—and his later life would be divided between the affairs of his estate and the affairs of his locality. On the Bench, until County Councils came into existence, he would have his share in local government as well as in the administration of justice,

The squire on his farm—from the Great Exhibition catalogue, 1851

and Quarter Sessions would see him gathered with his brother gentry in the market town. While the gentlemen attended to local politics, their families would be shopping; the shopkeepers depended heavily on the patronage of 'County people'. There might be a subscription ball in the evening at the Assembly Rooms which had been built, probably at 'the County's' expense, for 'the County's' convenience. Entertaining, either after this fashion or in their own houses, made up a great deal of the gentry's life. Great events apart—such as the birth of an heir, an heir's coming-of-age, or a marriage—there was a continual round of social activity between neighbouring country houses, though the

49

range of visiting, except where a stay overnight or longer was intended, was limited by the distance horses could comfortably travel in a day.

The building of the railways, the prosperity of the third quarter of the century, the general widening of the national horizons, began to break down the self-sufficiency of country life. London came within an hour or two's reach, and blocks of 'flats' were built where a family could have a London establishment without the expense of a house. Foreign travel became more attractive and easier. Something like an enlarged version of the Grand Tour began to emerge, taking in, particularly, the Colonies and the United States. For the sportsman, big-game hunting became possible. For relaxation and invalidism there were continental watering-places; for the active, the Alps. One effect of these wider opportunities was a much wider marriage market. In the later nineteenth century ancient families might readily be infused with new vigour and new money by the importation of American heiresses.

But even with all this wide field before him, the country gentleman's chief preoccupations were local. His position depended on his estate, which he neglected at his peril. It was essentially a base for a style of life, not a commercial undertaking, and even in times of great prosperity the return on capital employed was very low. But it yielded leisure, comfort, social position, very great personal liberty. The landowner who chose to observe the conventions of his class could be a respected figure among his neighbours, which was all that many men asked for. The landowner who did not—and the landed families were rich in eccentricity— might not be respected, but so long as he kept within the law and his own finances no one could prevent him from going his own way. Ambition, if a man had it, could be satisfied in politics, the services, or the Church—perhaps even in a profession, though that was slightly eccentric except for some one who really had no money of his own. There was no reason for the gentry to envy anyone on earth and the exhausting middle-class race to 'better oneself' was something which they could afford to regard with a good deal of scorn. All in all they had a life which was the freest and in many other ways the most agreeable ever known in England, which explains the perennial attraction of becoming a landed gentleman for anyone wealthy enough to do so.

In theory the gentry justified their privileges by disinterested public service and devoted care for the interests of their dependants. The theory was fairly new—it would probably have surprised most of the squires of Georgian and Regency England—but it did something to satisfy the stirrings of newly aroused social consciences and it had some effect in practice: enough, at any rate, to cast a rosy glow round the landowning class which was extremely gratifying to themselves, their admirers and their emulators. 'What a salutary and harmonizing influence', wrote a clergyman of the seventies, 'does a man of this sort give to a remote part of a remote county. Certainly there is no character in the world like that of an English country gentleman with adequate means, refined tastes, and, better still, endowed with religious instincts and principles.'

Whether the somewhat spurious glamour which surrounded the country gentleman was entirely a good thing, in the circumstances of late Victorian England, is open to question. The country was threatened by formidable industrial competition from abroad, and with the population heavily dependent on imported food the threat was potentially deadly. Yet the highest social prestige was still attached to people and institutions that had nothing to do with industry or trade at all, and the upper classes of society had an outlook that belonged to the past rather than the future, to the country rather than the town.

3 Farmers and their men

The gentry owned the land, the farmers rented it, the labourers worked it. This was the normal pattern of English agriculture under Victoria, and it was fairly new. Its distinctive feature was the separation between ownership and cultivation. There had once been a fair number of yeomen, farming their own land on some considerable scale, merging upwards into the gentry, but they had long dwindled, and the collapse of rural prosperity after the French wars had more or less finished them. The smallholders of the ancient common fields had been enclosed away over a very long period, and particularly fast in the late eighteenth and early nineteenth centuries. Some of their descendants had prospered as tenant farmers, some had gone to town, most had become labourers with no rights of cultivation beyond the garden hedge. Rural England had gone through a series of social revolutions of which the latest was quite recent.

'Reapers are very lightly clothed. The men cast their coats at least, and
many their waistcoats too. If his hat be laid aside, its place is taken by
the night cap. The women wear caps, not bonnets, and their nether
garments will incommode them the less in stooping, when cutting with
the sickle, if tied under the knee with the garter . . . Long gowns are
now in fashion . . . but the old short gown is the most convenient dress,
in every respect for a reaper.' Henry Stephens, *The Book of the Farm,*
II, 2nd ed. 1852

Squire and farmer, from an engraving after John Leech, 1851. 'If the farming men now and then mix with the landowners in their field sports, it is upon a footing of understood inferiority, and the association exists only out of doors, or in the public room of an inn after a cattle-show or an election. The difference in manners of the two classes does not admit of anything like social and family intercourse.' W. Johnston, *England as it is*, 1851

This upheaval in rural society was one result of the changes which had been wrought in English farming during the eighteenth century and which went on in the nineteenth, especially in the prosperous third quarter of the century. These changes were nearly all in favour of the large farmer, so that all the time small farms were growing fewer and large farms more numerous, though the process was not on such a scale as to make any very drastic difference in the number of farmers, which seems to have stayed somewhere just under 225,000 for most of the reign. Most will have been small men working 100 acres or less, by the labour of themselves and their families. The small 'working farmer' was particularly common in the Lake District and North Lancashire, where such men as were employed lived in the farmhouses until they married and then very often set up on their own on their own savings and their brides'. In parts of Yorkshire, on the other hand, and in East Anglia and the Cotswolds, there were large farmers, long established, who farmed several hundred acres, employed a good many men, and lived in some style.

The small farmer, scratching a living from a few acres of land, was scarcely above the labourers either in education or in general manner of life. Nor were larger farmers usually men of culture or broad views, though they might lead a life of roughish comfort and plenty. 'Farmers of the ordinary class', wrote W. Johnston in 1850, 'generally divide their time between the labours of their calling, and amusements with which neither mental cultivation nor refinement of taste have much to do'. Some amusements—field sports mostly—they were allowed to share with the gentry, but 'on a footing of understood inferiority, and the association exists only out of doors, or in the public room of an inn after an election'. Moreover, this kind of tolerance did not often extend to the shooting of game, and strict preserving was a fairly common source of ill-feeling between landlords and tenants. Hunting, on the other hand, tended to draw the two sides together, and the farmers were allowed to share in it. But on the whole the difference in manners between the two classes was much too great for any close social intercourse, even if the family pride of the gentry would have allowed it. The clergy, though not necessarily much richer

Farmers at home, from an engraving after Thomas Seccombe, about 1875. Right at the end of mid-Victorian farming prosperity, these two are evidently enjoying hot toddy in the farmhouse kitchen

Churning Butter

GRAPHIC ILLUSTRATIO

SHEWING THEIR UTILITY TO MAN, IN THEIR SERVICES

Agricultural

Published by THOMAS VARTY, 31, Strand, London.

Slaughter

The Butcher

Cooking

Solid Food

Cheese

Liquid Food

ANIMALS,

E AND USES AFTER DEATH.

Cutlery & Turnery

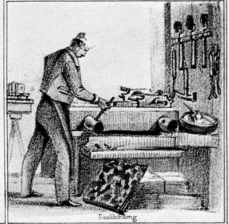

Bookbinding

Candles

Library   For Light

than the larger farmers—some clergymen may have been a good deal poorer—shared the attitudes of the gentry, and they were not on very close terms with the farmers either. Many, in fact, knew the labourers much better because the farmer, again in Johnston's words, 'frequently desires to manifest a surly independence of the parson', so that the parson's hat might more often be hung up in a cottage than in a farmhouse.

The farmers took little part in running local affairs. Under the old Quarter Sessions system there was not much opening for them, and there is little evidence that they took much interest. They might serve as guardians of the poor or as churchwardens, but it was beyond them, socially and educationally, to become magistrates. Nor, as a rule, were they much concerned with national politics, being happy enough, except in moments of uncommon stress, to vote as their landlords wished. In Norfolk a tenant farmer, C. S. Reade, was in Parliament for a good many years up to 1881, but that was altogether unusual. Over the countryside generally the passing of the yeoman, owning land as well as farming it, had left a gap in the social system which the tenant farmer did not adequately fill: his standing was uneasy and isolated.

Partly, no doubt, the trouble was the farmer's attitude to education. He might be prepared to have his daughters polished up a little, but he saw small benefit in book learning for his sons, especially if schooling looked expensive. In the fifties and sixties, when the grammar schools were acknowledged to be failing, a number of 'county schools' were set up, intended particularly for farmers' sons. One was at West Buckland in Devon, another at Framlingham and another at Cranleigh.

The county schools were proprietary boarding schools (see Chapter 7). To keep the fees down the boys lived in hostels and ate centrally, instead of being spread about in masters' houses, as at the ancient public schools. They were set up for farmers but not by farmers, and the schools' sponsors found that farmers were inclined to look on such things as new books, expensive apparatus and well-paid staff as extravagances. Even if they were willing to believe that the education and the living conditions were worth the price asked for them, they were apt to think they could get all their sons required without paying so much for it. 'Many of them', said the Report of the Schools Enquiry Commission in 1868, 'do not yet appreciate airy and well arranged

schoolrooms and dormitories, single beds, abundant washing apparatus, any more than the study of French or Euclid.' An illuminating comment, this, on the way prosperous Victorian farmers were accustomed to live, as well as on their view of education.

Towards the end of the seventies the farmers of England began to feel the impact of foreign competition, especially in the shape of imports of American grain. It was all the worse because it coincided with a run of bad seasons. In the past the bad seasons would have raised the price of grain and the Corn Laws would have prevented foreigners from underselling. By the seventies the Corn Laws had gone and the prairie farmers, newly linked by rail with the Atlantic ports, could undersell in a big way. On 31st December 1879 a

The village schoolroom, from an engraving after C. O. Murray, 1879. A school, perhaps, of the type described by Flora Thompson in *Lark Rise to Candleford*: '. . . a small grey one-storeyed building, standing at the cross-roads at the entrance to the village'

'One of the pleasantest forms of entertainment is a well-arranged picnic (if only a fine day be selected), while nothing is calculated to give greater dissatisfaction than a badly-managed one. To have chosen the wrong people . . . , to have given people wrong seats in the various vehicles, or to have too many ladies in the party, are all too often fatal errors.' Mrs Beeton gives £3 6s 1d (£3.29½) as the cost of a picnic for twenty. *Mrs Beeton's Book of Household Management.* 1895 edition

Monmouthshire farmer wrote in his diary: 'Being the last day of the year which is a very good thing it is. This year 1879 has been one of the wettest years any living man can remember and a very disasterous one for agriculture. Having a very bad yeald of corn & sheep rotten & doing very bad.'

The shaky grammar and spelling of this extract betray the educational limitations of even the larger farmers of the day, for the diarist, William Till, had spent a couple of years at a boarding school (1868–70) before, at the age of fifteen, he joined his father on the farm, which consisted of about 500 acres of arable and pasture land at Caerwent in Monmouthshire. By the time he was keeping his diary he had taken over the running of the farm. On an ordinary day he would get up early and, as he put it, 'set the men to rights'. Then he might spend the day in work about the farm—or he might not. He shot, he fished, he dug out badgers, he sang with the village glee club, and he visited friends and relations. Of one typical evening he records 'had tea & sundry games of wist . . . lost –/9 spent a very injoyable evening. Arrived home after a pleasant ride 3:15 a.m.'

The homespun nature of country amusements may be judged from the record of a picnic in the hills on an evening in July 1880. Thirty-five people (30 'young people'; 5 'married'), having had tea, 'began dancing to the music of Tom the Fiddler—kept it up till 11-30 p.m. . . . didn't get to bed till 1 o'clock a.m.' They paid the fiddler 10s. (50p) and a servant girl 3s. 6d. (17½p). Till described it as 'one of the jolliest sprees imaginable.' In general, the life which this farmer's diary reveals was simple and strenuous, both in work and pleasure. It was more circumscribed than the

At a village cricket match, from a painting by John Reid, 1878. Smock frocks are still worn by the labourers. Presumably the young man in the background is a gentleman; hence his cap and other attire

better documented life of the gentry and, no doubt, less cultivated, although Till was sufficiently interested in Roman coins found on his farm to form a collection of them, but there were points of similarity, especially in the taste for hearty physical exercise, often with a dash of blood. Probably the life of a substantial tenant farmer under Victoria was a good deal like the life led by the smaller gentry under the Georges, before rising wealth and easier travel had combined to broaden their horizons and alter their ideas of what a gentleman's life should be.

A few farmers were rich: many were comfortably off. Of the people whom they employed—the labourers—the one outstanding common characteristic was that they were all poor. Cash wages in some districts, just before the Crimean War, had fallen as low as 6s. (30p) or 7s. 6d. (37½p). Over the next fifty years they rose, though not steadily because they varied with the general prosperity of farming. By the end of the century it was calculated by Wilson Fox that labourers' wages in the Midlands and the eastern counties were about forty per cent greater than in 1850: in the south and south-west, fifty-seven per cent. There were great differences from one part of the country to another, but by 1900 the weekly earnings of an ordinary farm labourer, taking account of allowances in kind, might run from about 15s. (75p) in purely agricultural counties to 20s. (£1) in Durham and Northumberland, where industry and mining were close enough to force up farm wages. Pay was always better near London and the factories than it was in, say, Somerset or Berkshire. Cowmen, shepherds and carters would always get more than ordinary labourers, especially where animals of great value were reared, but their pay was low compared with what they could get in towns, and their duties were more arduous than the unskilled men's, because the needs of animals take no account of their guardians' convenience.

Of the allowance in kind which made up some part of farm labourers' earnings the most important was usually a cottage held on a very low rent or no rent at all—and on a very insecure tenure. There might be beer, cider or food at harvest time, free carting of fuel, an allowance of milk or, in the north, half a ton of potatoes a year. These things varied very much from place to place and where their value was greatest, cash wages were lowest, so that there was no real gain from them. Money, in any case, was the labourer's greatest need. He could usually feed himself, with a pig behind his cottage and the produce of his garden, but how was

A 'hiring' fair; Burford, in Oxfordshire, from a late-Victorian photograph. An annual fair of the kind at which the countryman, as well as amusing himself, could seek a different job, for which, traditionally, he would be hired by the year

he to buy clothing and especially boots? Payments for piece-work and harvesting, therefore, were extremely important to him. They were calculated according to all sorts of different local customs, and they might be worth as much as £4 or £5 a year.

The utmost that could be expected on a farm labourer's income, if he had a decent cottage, good health and not too many children, was a certain frugal comfort, which would depend very much on his wife's skill and strength of character. It was all too easy, especially for the aged and the sick, to fall into utter wretchedness, and Johnston, writing in 1850 when agriculture was depressed, remarked: 'A kind of Irish fate seems to hang over the lowest grade of the population, and they accept labour and sorrow, overcrowding and unhealthiness, as their destined portion.' A Dorset clergyman, at the same date, described the country people as 'patient, enduring, thankful, and civil; but, either from extreme poverty, or the habit from earliest youth of seeking

their fuel in the woods or fields, they are rather given to pilfering'. Another clergyman of the same county—the county of Tolpuddle, where labourers were notoriously badly off—said, 'Let the labouring class see that they depend upon the observance of the decencies of life, and moral and religious conduct, for employment and the means of comfortable living—let them thus experience the respective consequences of virtue and of vice.'

Reverend gentlemen might speak of 'the decencies of life', but how was Hodge to get to know anything about them when, all too often, he had not even a decent house to live in? Many cottages had one room downstairs, one above. Few had more than two bedrooms. They were unlikely to have been very well built in the first place, and they might have been neglected since, so that they would be damp, cold and draughty as well as overcrowded. Farm labourers' housing was a scandal for years—it was noticed, for instance, in a well-known *Punch* drawing of the sixties—and it was very thoroughly investigated by a Royal Commission, on which the Prince of Wales served, which reported in 1885. 'You will find', said one witness, 'between the Mendips and

Overcrowding in the country: a labourer's cottage, from an engraving in the *Graphic*, 1872. 'Insufficient sleeping accommodation, defective ventilation, paucity of light, and almost utter absence of drainage render the labourer's cottage a source of demoralisation against which the influence of the clergyman cannot contend

the fashionable watering-place known as Weston-super-Mare that you can hardly call the dwellings cottages, for some of them are only lean-to roofs up against the wall.' In one room of such a hovel, the witness said, he had seen eleven children and their parents. And there was plenty more evidence to the same effect from all over the country, but particularly from west Somerset and north Devon—remote rural areas where the draw of the towns, that great force for improving farm labourers' lives, had not been much felt.

Conditions of this sort stirred some landowners to action. When the Prince of Wales bought Sandringham early in the sixties the estate was run-down, remote and neglected, because the previous owner had lived there very little, only visiting occasionally for the shooting. In twenty years or so the Prince put up more than seventy new cottages, each with three bedrooms and two living rooms. Other landowners all over the country did the same sort of thing, building pairs

Baking day in a Warwickshire cottage. 'The porch, the tank and the oven, which ought, as Mr Disraeli says, to belong to every rustic homestead are not forgotten in building new cottages on well-managed estates.' (*The Illustrated London News*, 4th May 1872)

or short rows of cottages in stone or brick (against the timber and wattle-and-daub of previous centuries), and marking them with crest or cypher, such as the coroneted B on the Bedford estates or the 'black-letter' S on Prebendary

A child bird-scarer, from an engraving after John Leech

Stephenson's cottages and farmhouses at Lympsham in Somerset. Generally speaking, conditions were best where villages were in the hands of one owner. In 'open' villages where many small owners held the various properties, and especially where farmers were responsible for their men's cottages, the housing was at its most deplorable. In these overcrowded tumbledown houses the offence to morality, to the Victorian mind, was the gravest of many offences against ordinary ideas of civilized life, and the most that could be said for country cottages in general was that the overcrowding was not quite so bad as in town slums, because most families had more than one room to live in.

Many villages were tiny, inbred communities. In the fens near Downham, Norfolk, there was a place called Southery where in 1876 there were said to be only three surnames in the parish, and parallel cases could have been found in other remote, isolated districts such as, for instance, the low-lying 'moors' of Somerset or Romney Marsh. And in a labourer's life there was scant room for education, so that the 'yokel's' stupidity, ignorance and gullibility were a stock joke among townees. Certainly until well on in the century many farm labourers, probably most, must have been to a greater or less degree illiterate, because until the Act of 1870 made provision for a school within reach of every child in the land it was a matter of chance whether a country child could get to school or not. A good many squires and parsons saw to it that schools were built, often at their own expense, partly as a result of the general quickening of the social conscience and partly to make sure that the poor were taught proper notions of religion and morality. As an inscription at Shalbourne, Wiltshire, puts it: 'A.D. 1843— This school was built for the purpose of giving a bible education to the Children of the Poor.' But there was no compulsion on the gentry to build or on the 'children of the poor' to attend.

For the villagers, indeed, compulsion was the other way; school had to take second place to earning. 'I once went to school for a week', said a farmer's boy of 1850. 'I know that twice ten is twenty, because I have heard other boys say so. I cannot read.' He was twelve and had probably been at work for four years or so, since boys of eight could earn 4d. (1½p) a day at scaring birds off newly-sown corn, or by helping their fathers with odd jobs, and from that age on they would be at work whenever work could be found. As one boy put it, 'When I am not at work I do not often get bread and

A country labourer and his family: an idealised portrait from Mary Russell Mitford, *Our Village,* 1879 edition

meat for dinner. . . . . I had rather work than play, you get most victuals when you work.'

Women worked in the fields as well, though the practice was pretty generally deplored and diminished as time went on. A woman of 1850 said she had had thirteen children, of whom seven grew up, and she had been accustomed to field work for eleven hours a day at haytime and harvest. In the autumn she would go out gleaning, perhaps from two in the morning to seven in the evening, perhaps as much as seven miles from home, and she would take three daughters (aged ten, fifteen and eighteen) with her. For this effort, she would reckon six bushels of corn a very good reward. Such habits had a disastrous effect on home life. 'When the wife returns . . .', says Johnston, 'she has to look after her children, and her husband may have to wait for his supper. He may come home tired and wet; he finds his wife has arrived but just before him; she must give her attention to the children; there is no fire, no supper, no comfort, and he goes to the beer-shop.' In 1864 an East Anglian parson visited a young woman who was dying—'a victim of *field work*, a disgrace to the county'. Thirty years later, in parts of Norfolk, Cambridgeshire and south Lincolnshire, gangs of women and girls were still being hired out to farmers at busy times, and in the north labourers' daughters were still working on the land.

The best thing a cottager's daughter could hope for was to go into service in a good family, and when she was between ten and fifteen years old her parents would try to place her. The Census Report of 1891 remarked on the fewness of women, in country districts, at all ages from ten upwards. It also said that almost one-third of all girls in the country, between the ages of fifteen and twenty, were in service, and about one in every eight over the age of ten. These figures indicate the intense pressure to get away from the villages, the demand for servants, and the very limited openings for women outside domestic service.

Life in service could be dreary and laborious, especially where there was only one maid. The lists of servants' duties given in Victorian works on household management are intimidating. Employers certainly expected hard work, for the idea that the lower classes (or the middle classes, for that matter) should do anything but work hard did not enter anyone's head. But in a good household the maid's job had solid advantages. A girl was well fed, clothed and housed. She would see something of a wider world and she would get some idea of how to run a house. If she were in some great mansion she would have her place—however lowly—in the ordered, ceremonious life of the servants' hall, where distinctions of rank, from butler down to kitchen-maid, were meticulously observed, and she would gain some idea of good behaviour. There was always the hope that she might become an 'upper servant', though these generally came from the farmers' families rather than the cottagers', and she

A woman labourer, from an engraving after W. H. J. Boot, 1879

Maids in a London hotel, from a
photograph of 1892. 'The chief
characteristics of the new hotels
are the ubiquitous German
waiters and the sameness of the
food.' T. H. S. Escott, about 1880.

might marry some steady young man who would take her from poverty towards the comfort of the lower middle class. And she would be a good catch as a wife if she were a careful girl, for the Royal Commission on Labour, in 1894, concluded that women in domestic service earned some £50 a year; girls, £28. From earnings of that order saving was perfectly possible, though a good deal of the money found its way back to the impoverished villages, for girls in service remembered their parents. But there was the danger, realized all too often, that marriage would drag a girl back to the dreariness of cottage life, with too much work, too many children, too little money and the fear of the workhouse at the end of it all.

However great the hardship of the life of the country poor, it was at least less grinding from the middle of the century onwards and, on the whole, things grew better rather than worse. To take one example, by the end of the century the labourer might be riding to work on his bicycle rather than trudging on foot, and the fact that he could buy a bicycle would have astonished his grandfather no less than the existence of the machine itself. Moreover, cheap imported food, though from one point of view it imperilled his livelihood, from another standpoint worked as much to his advantage as to the advantage of the poor generally, for he had more and better things to eat than the bread, potatoes, fat bacon and beans of earlier times.

Most important of all, the doors of escape from the countryside opened wider and more attractively as time went on. In the past, almost the only possibility had been enlistment: very much a last resort when the recruit signed on for life, cut himself off from his friends by doing so, and lived in peril of the lash. Consequently, only the poorest and most desperate enlisted, which accounts for the fact that at the Census of 1851, just after the Irish famine, thirty-seven per cent of the men in the ranks of the Army came from Ireland, and Ireland was at all times a prolific recruiting ground, though the proportion of Irishmen in the ranks dropped greatly as time passed.

By about the seventies, conditions of army life had been greatly improved. Short-service engagements had been brought in, a month's furlough was allowed to 'well-conducted' soldiers in the winter, the officers were taking more interest in their men's welfare, and in general a few years in the Army was becoming something which a respectable man could contemplate.

Enlistment was one possibility. Emigration was another. As penal transportation ceased, the colonies became more attractive to honest men, and as sailing ships gave way to steam the discomfort and danger of long voyages grew less. The discovery of gold in California and Australia in the middle of the century drew many adventurers; others, more sober, could find land cheap or free in the United States and elsewhere. The numbers who went abroad varied with the state of employment in England, and of course they were not all countrymen, but during the eighties 1,500,000 people of English and Welsh origin—this excludes the Scots and Irish—left the United Kingdom for places outside Europe, and that was the culmination of a process that had long been going on; nor did it cease with the eighties. Emigration, in fact, reached its greatest figures between 1911 and 1913.

But the countryman might seek his fortune much closer at hand, and the Census figures show in what numbers he did so. In 1851, 1,200,000 men and 143,000 women were reported working on farms; in 1901, 700,000 and 12,000. Whatever anyone might say about the horrors of the towns, their unhealthiness, and the dissatisfactions of factory life, the villager was ready to take the risk. By the time Queen Victoria died, country life in England, with all its habits of thought and its scale of values, was looking more and more like an anachronistic island disappearing beneath the waves of the rising industrial tide. However great the sentimental attraction of the land might be for the ruling classes, matters were very different for Hodge. For him the railway line to town was the route to better things.

A farm labourer in a West-country traditional smock

72

4 The growth of towns

In the early fifties a labourer, dissatisfied with 8*s*. 6*d*. (42½p) a week, left an East Anglian village and tramped to London, 3*s*. 6*d*. (17½p) in his pocket, to find a better job. He sought out a cousin, already settled as a carpenter, and found a horse-keeping job with Pickfords. They paid him a guinea (£1.05) a week.

From Pickfords, still working with horses, he moved to the Great Northern Railway and rose to be managing foreman, with forty or fifty men under him, at their depot near the East India Docks. He had a great scorn for born Londoners and a great belief in countrymen, especially from his own district. Over the years he placed a good many, either under himself or elsewhere, so that he became something like an employment agency for people from his old neighbourhood. And if those whom he brought in were successful they encouraged and helped others to come, and so on.

In the eighties, ageing and rheumaticky (he did not come to London until he was thirty-two), the foreman retired on a comfortable railway pension. It would be even more comfortable in the country, so he left his house and garden at Blackwall and went back to end his days in the place where he had been born. He told his story to one of Charles Booth's investigators, and Booth used it, in *Life and Labour in London*, to show how countrymen came to London and, no doubt, to the other large towns of the kingdom. In particular, he wanted to show that they did not all drift aimlessly into dead-end jobs at the bottom of the labour market.

The countryman could usually look for much better things. To start with, he rarely came to town haphazard. He generally knew of someone who could help him while he was looking for a job, or actually get him into one. Nor did he necessarily find a job difficult to get especially if, like horse-keeping, it called for country skills. Employers liked the 'thick-set, red-faced men of good medium height and enormous strength', as Flora Thompson has described the farm labourers whom she knew in the eighties, especially in contrast with the sickly, under-sized people of the towns whom so many Victorian social commentators remarked upon. And the difference in pay was so great that the countryman, right from the start, was almost bound to gain from his move, even allowing for the higher cost of living in town.

With the penny post the advantages and possibilities of town life became better and better known in the country. Booth, writing late in the century, considered that 'one of

The development of rail travel: the waiting room at Fenchurch Street station in London. From the painting 'Parting Words' by F. B. Barwell, 1859

(Preceding page) Bradford in 1873

the most powerful and efficient migration agencies is . . . the letters written home by the country girl settled in domestic service in the great town'. That, of course, was after the Education Act of 1870 had added widespread literacy to the cheapness of the postal services, thus greatly increasing the number of potential letter writers. The vicar of East Dereham in Norfolk recorded in his diary that the number of letters passing through the local post office rose from 7,000 a week in 1873 to 25,000 in 1876. He put it down to the rise in population, but the new schools may also have had something to do with it.

As the countryman came to know more about the town, so it became easier for him to get there. George Stephenson, according to Smiles, very early predicted the time 'when it would be cheaper for a working man to make a journey by railway than to walk on foot'. The railways at length woke up to the potentialities of the market for third-class travel— not without a certain amount of legislative prodding—and by the seventies Stephenson's prediction had come true. The man from the country no longer had to tramp for days to get to town. Even more important, perhaps, he could sometimes afford to visit friends in town and see for himself what things were like there.

Many villagers, until well on in Victoria's reign, were totally uneducated and for them the move to town was a formidable undertaking if, indeed, their minds were ever stirred to contemplate it. But village schools were spreading, and after 1870 the law required one within the reach of every child. They might provide only the barest primary instruction, but that was more than many children had had the chance of before. Even more important, all were now required to submit themselves to it. The question whether to send a child to school or not was no longer left with poverty-stricken parents as it had been in the past.

In a few minds schooling, even of a meagre kind, worked upon lively intelligence, provoking discontent with the limitations of village life, opening up prospects hitherto unglimpsed, suggesting even, perhaps, questioning of the unquestionable—was the social order of the countryside divinely ordained, immutable, inescapable? Flora Thompson has described how the more intelligent village youngsters, their minds thus stirred, looked with lively hope towards the towns. Even the dull were no longer quite the unlettered simpletons they otherwise would have been. Everyone had the rudiments of the mental equipment needed to cope with nineteenth-century life.

Thus throughout Victoria's reign increasingly powerful forces were at work to persuade country people that they would do better for themselves in town. By the time the 1851 Census was taken there were more people, for the first time in history, in the towns of England and Wales than in the country. There was then only a bare majority, but fifty years later, at the Census of 1901, 25,000,000 people (about fifty per cent more than the total population of England and Wales in 1851) were living in the towns and only 7,500,000 outside.

The new town-dwellers, of course, did not all come from

the English countryside. The Scots came, especially to the towns of the north, to London and to the mines, and by 1900 there were over 250,000 people of Scots birth in England and Wales. At a lower social level, as a rule, and in much greater numbers came the Irish, especially in the forties when Irish distress was at its worst. Later, they were more inclined to go to the United States, where many had friends and relations. There were about 600,000 people of Irish birth in England and Wales in the sixties. The figure fell as time went on, but it bore a rising proportion to the falling population of Ireland itself.

The Irish came mostly to big towns close to their ports of landing, mainly in Lancashire and Cheshire, and to London. They were nearly all from a countryside much more backward and poverty-stricken than the English, and they usually took the roughest sort of unskilled labour. The Irish quarter of Liverpool was described by Hippolyte Taine, in the sixties, as 'the nethermost circle of Hell', and throughout

Leaving Ireland: waiting for a train at Galway. Engraving from *Punch*, 1852

A Jewish old-clothes man, from
an engraving of 1861 after an
early photograph. In 1850, before
the great immigration, later in
the century, from Eastern Europe,
there were probably about 35,000
Jews in England, of whom some
18,000–20,000 lived in London,
chiefly in the City and East
End; Westminster and
Marylebone; and Southwark.
V. D. Lipman, *Social History of
the Jews in England 1850–1950*,
1954

the century the Irish were close to the heart of the problem
of poverty.

From about 1880 onward Jews, driven by persecution from
their homes in Russian Poland, began to flock into London
and a few other towns. During the eighties about 30,000
came, and by 1901 nearly 83,000 people from Russia or
Russian Poland were living in England and Wales. These
would nearly all have been Jews, who had long overtaken
the Germans as the most numerous foreign community in
England. They were heavily concentrated in small districts,
especially the East End of London. In Stepney in 1901 there
were 54,000 foreigners in a population of 200,000, and a high
proportion must have been immigrant Jews.

They came mostly by way of Hamburg or ports on the
Baltic and usually landed desperately poor, though not
always friendless, for relations might be waiting for them.
Coming from centuries of persecution, they had little sense
of civic duty, for the State had always been an enemy, but
their family feeling was intense and their determination to
better themselves indomitable.

This determination, which was sometimes coupled with
the intellectual training of Talmudic studies, made them
formidable competitors of the working classes of the English
towns, particularly the feckless Irish who resembled them
in their poverty but in nothing else. Beatrice Potter, contri-
buting to Booth's investigations, called the immigrant Jews
'a race of brainworkers competing with a class of manual
labourers', and she described how they would work for the
first opportunity to turn from manual labour to some form
of trading.

It might be carried on, at first, in circumstances of the
utmost squalor and without too nice a regard for the law,
but success would bring solid *bourgeois* respectability and
comfort—jewels for the wife, chicken for Sunday dinner,
earnest planning of the children's future. The rising business man might take his glass of rum and shrub and he
might play cards, but he would not go to the pub. If he had a
vice, it would probably be gambling, but his interests would
very likely be cultural and artistic; he might take season
tickets for the People's Palace. 'In short,' Beatrice Potter
concluded, 'he has become a law-abiding and self-respecting
citizen of our great metropolis, and feels himself the equal
of a Montefiore or a Rothschild.'

And, it might be added, of all those who came into the
towns under Victoria, the immigrant Jews took most readily

to urban life. Not for them the rural hankerings of the Englishman, so often translated, in prosperity or old age, into actual physical withdrawal into the countryside. The Jews accepted town life as natural and, as they prospered, enriched it. The musical and artistic life of English towns, especially in the north, owes a great deal to Jewish influence.

Apart from drawing people from the countryside and from abroad, the towns grew by natural increase, though it was severely checked by appalling mortality among babies and children. The 1851 Census gave the 'mean lifetime' in Liverpool and Manchester as twenty-five years and reported that only about forty-five per cent of the babies born in Liverpool reached the age of twenty.

This was largely because the growth of towns on anything like the Victorian scale was something previously unimagined and it caused problems which no one had ever had to face before. A 'town' to previous generations—outside London—had been small enough to be manageable. Like Trollope's Barchester, it might possess 'two pumps, three hotels, ten shops, fifteen beerhouses, a beadle, and a marketplace', and a quarter of an hour's walk in any direction from the centre would probably take the inhabitants into the country. Corrupt these places often were and in their backstreets tumbledown and dirty, but they were stable, ancient communities who through long use knew how to manage their own affairs after their own fashion, which often enough showed little trace of the reforming spirit supposed to have been let loose by the Municipal Corporations Act of 1835. At Rye in Sussex, for example, two brothers-in-law alternated as Mayor for twenty years, and a spell in jail for perjury failed to blast the career of one of them, because his power was based on being the largest employer of labour in the town.

Such towns had at least some system of government and some corporate personality, but the new manufacturing towns, generally speaking, had neither. They grew almost with the speed and with very much the character of mining camps, and if any ancient corporation did exist it was apt to be overwhelmed. To take a few random examples, Salford between 1861 and 1881 grew by 72 per cent, Leicester by 80 per cent, Liverpool by 24·5 per cent and Middlesbrough, which in 1831 had 383 people, had by 1871 more than 100 times as many. Nearly all this growth went on without any planning at all so that Widnes, for example, had in 1865 no public sewer for its 10,000 inhabitants, and eleven years later the vicar complained that the local manufacturers of sodium carbonate, using the Leblanc process, seemed to think they had a right to stifle him, crumble the slates on the church roof and drive away prospective curates.

Life in the towns was mostly for the young. People came young to look for work, many died young, and the elderly were inclined to move away, particularly if they had prospered. The result was that there were far more people between the ages of fifteen and forty-five than there were in the country, but at all other ages there were fewer, except for children under five. After five the number of children was sharply cut down by death. And these figures are not taken from one of the familiar tales of early Victorian horror, such as the report on the health of towns of 1842. They come from the report of the Census of 1891.

The greatest problem of the towns was to keep their people alive, and throughout the century it was never entirely solved. A building in Hampstead, as an inscription on its wall records, 'was erected by voluntary contributions for a dispensary and soup kitchen . . . as a thank-offering to ALMIGHTY GOD for his special mercy in sparing this parish during the visitation of cholera in the year 1849'. Cholera was a recurring risk of town life until the eighties, which is not really surprising when it is considered that as late as 1871 the waterworks service in England and Wales only employed 3,347 people. In the same year, about 23,000 people were killed by smallpox.

It was these appalling epidemics—especially cholera—which, more than anything else, brought energetic municipal government into being and made people realize that rates would have to be paid and irksome bye-laws passed—and kept—if the towns were ever to become moderately healthy. But many of the Victorian acts dealing with public health, housing, municipal finance and so on were permissive rather than mandatory, so that towns differed very much according as they had energetic citizens, willing to tax themselves, or not. At Birmingham, in the often-quoted phrase of Joseph Chamberlain, measures were taken to have the town 'parked, paved, assized, marketed, Gas-and-Watered, and *improved*' while he was himself mayor in the mid-seventies. At Wednesbury, on the other hand, as late as 1897, a street subsided into a yawning, burning chasm caused by fire in the coal measures, and nothing was done

London Bridge, 1872, from an engraving after Gustave Doré. 'It is curious to see the eager faces that crowd to the sides of a steamer from the ocean, when London Bridge is fairly outlined against the horizon, and the dome of St Paul's rises behind. This is the view of London which is familiar to all civilised peoples.' Gustave Doré and Blanchard Jerrold, *London, A Pilgrimage*, 1872

CHOLERA.

THE
DUDLEY BOARD OF HEALTH,

HEREBY GIVE NOTICE, THAT IN CONSEQUENCE OF THE

Church-yards at Dudley

Being so full, no one who has died of the
CHOLERA will be permitted to be buried
after *SUNDAY* next, (To-morrow) in either
of the Burial Grounds of St. *Thomas's*, or
St. *Edmund's*, in this Town.

All Persons who die from CHOLERA, must for the future
be buried in the Church-yard at Nethertor.

BOARD of HEALTH, DUDLEY.

for months because the Corporation was disputing liability
with a local company. Not even the death of their night
watchman, who fell into the hole and was suffocated, could
jolt them into emergency action. They had their ratepayers
to think of.

At the heart of the problem of public health lay overcrowding. There were never enough houses, especially for the very
poor. Lord Shaftesbury, speaking in 1885 after fifty years'
experience, said it was worse than ever in London and very
bad in the provinces. It might be a matter of too many people
in too few rooms, like the house in Spitalfields which in the
eighties had an average of seven people in each of nine
rooms, and in no room more than one bed. It might be caused
by too many houses in too little space, as in parts of Birmingham before Chamberlain set to work. Very often there were
both troubles.

Some very bad slum property in London was pulled down
to make way for railways, with their termini and goods
yards, and the building of warehouses got rid of more, but
measures like this did not solve the problem because the
people who moved had to find somewhere else to live. Since
they were very poor, what they moved into was apt to be no
better than what they had left: it might even be worse. The
blocks of 'model' dwellings which went up from the sixties
onwards were not for the poorest, and the days of municipal
housing schemes were far in the future.

The kind of houses that were built, as the towns grew, was

84

In 1850 about 331,000 people worked in factories in the cotton industry
in the United Kingdom, 189,000 were women and girls, and 15,000
(9,000 boys; 6,000 girls) were under 13. For the years 1850–59 cotton
goods accounted for 36 per cent of the country's total exports, and until
the Second World War they remained at the head of the percentages of
the total. P. Mathias, *The First Industrial Nation* 1969 and B. R.
Mitchell and Phyllis Deane, *Abstract of British Historical Statistics*,
1962

very much a matter for individual landlords' judgement. Some built houses intended from the first for working-class occupation, and very rude about them the Royal Commissioners of 1885 were. 'It is perhaps needless', they said in their report, 'to give a detailed description of the way in which many modern houses are run up for the working classes . . . "jerry building" is too well known . . . the houses are often built of the commonest materials, and with the worst workmanship, and are altogether unfit for people to live in, especially if they are a little rough in their ways. . . . It is quite certain that the working classes are largely housed in dwellings which would be unsuitable even if they were not overcrowded.'

Many of the houses of the poor were the cast-off dwellings of more prosperous people, for in all the large towns, as they grew, there was a constant flight of wealth from the centre to the suburbs. Great numbers of new houses were built but the old ones were not all knocked down. They became tenement houses, and where one family had lived in comfort —even affluence—under George IV, as many families as the place had rooms might live under the middle-aged or elderly Victoria. Late in the twentieth century it is possible to see, in many large English towns, successive belts of shabby property, once respectable, which, like the growth rings of a tree, mark the outward expansion of the town, with its wealthier inhabitants always at the leading edge.

Suburbs grew on a scale never before seen, which was only made possible by the spread of railways. Keats, no doubt, had walked every day from Hampstead to the Borough and back, but that was not what your mid-Victorian City man had to do. He caught his train, morning and evening, and he lived anything up to thirty or forty miles from his daily work. This was something which had never been possible before, and it set an entirely new pattern of middle-class life. Nor was it entirely confined to London, though commonest and most conspicuous there. The big provincial towns grew dormitory suburbs too, as for instance Birmingham near which, in the last ten years of the century, King's Norton and Northfield more than doubled their population.

Thus the growth of the great towns, especially London, generated growth in the country towns and villages round about, where the prosperous went to live. Samuel Smiles, in 1879, remarked on the number of new towns, of 10,000 or 20,000 people, which had sprung up round London in twenty years or so. Before suburban railways, the limit of daily

To combat the discomforts of travelling by horse-bus, De Tivoli's patent omnibus of 1860 was designed with 'separate well-ventilated compartments' for one person each, 'fitted like first-class railway carriages. A position at the back . . . is left undivided to contain four persons . . . and constitutes a second-class carriage.' (*The Illustrated London News*, 9th June 1860)

(Overleaf) 'An admirable picture of Ramsgate sands, "Life at the Sea Side" by W. P. Frith, R.A., lately engraved by the Art Union of London, has familiarised the scene to many.' Mackenzie Walcott, M.A. *A Guide to the South Coast of England*, 1859

travel had been set by horse transport, especially the horse bus, and the old suburbs did not run much further than Hampstead and Highgate on the north, Paddington and Kensington on the west, and Clapham and Brixton on the south—say, six miles or so from St Paul's. But as the lines came into the City—and Smiles spoke of 300 stations 'in actual use' within five miles of Charing Cross—the rail journey from Barnet, Watford, Richmond, Reigate and Erith became quicker than the bus ride from the 'old suburbs'. Guildford, Epsom, Dorking and other country towns came easily within reach of the City for those who could afford the fares, and a daily journey from the coast was perfectly practicable. 'Clapham and Bayswater', Smiles concluded, '. . . have become as it were parts of the great metropolis, and Brighton and Hastings are but the marine suburbs of London.'

That may have been an exaggeration, but there was no doubt that seaside towns and inland watering-places, under the joint impulse of rising middle-class prosperity and the

spread of railways, grew immensely fast. The Census of 1871 listed fifty-six of them, with a total population of 670,000. Londoners went to Margate, Ramsgate, Hastings and Brighton. Further off were Torquay and Torbay 'with the charms of an Italian lake' (the words of the Census Report, not of the town guide), the Welsh towns and 'to the north-east Scarborough, the fair mistress of that coast'. Since 1861 the inhabitants of the watering-places had increased their numbers by nineteen per cent—a faster rate of growth than in any but the fastest-growing industrial towns.

Watering places were sometimes created by landowners, as Eastbourne and Buxton were created by the Duke of Devonshire. Or they might be made by what one writer (T. H. S. Escott) called 'some go-ahead speculator, whether in bricks and mortar or in land'. The first necessity was for some one to recognize commercial possibilities in a fishing village with a beach or in a country town with a mineral

A Pullman dining-car on the Great Northern Railway, 1879, enabled a Leeds man to leave home after breakfast, have lunch on the train, spend three hours in London, dine at 6 or 7, and be home by midnight. 'Irregular dining hours, beyond all doubt, have shortened the lives of many prosperous and active men of business who were little past middle age. The Pullman Company therefore deserve our support in this department of their enterprise . . .' (*The Illustrated London News*, 22nd November 1879)

spring, lying on a line of railway within reasonably easy reach of some large town. Developing the resort would then be partly a matter of building and partly of advertising and public relations. A good way to start was to get the place recommended by the doctors, for people like to feel that what they fancy also does them good. Streets, shops, hotels would have to be built and the drainage seen to. There would have to be a promenade and no doubt a pier as well, and, a little back from the sea, pleasure gardens would appear with (in the seventies) a roller-skating rink and lawn tennis courts. The process was succinctly put down by the Rev. B. J. Armstrong in his diary when, in 1853, he wrote of Lowestoft: 'through the spirited exertions of Mr Peto, M.P., there is a beautiful pier, a grand esplanade, and a superb hotel, quite in the French style'. One or two fashionable preachers would add to the attractions of the town, for the watering-places were great centres of theological controversy among religious ladies, and it would be well if schools could be set up and gain a wide reputation, as they

Hydropathic Establishment, Matlock Bank, from *Thirty Views of Derbyshire*, 1869. 'Smedley's convalescent institution is a most imposing-looking building, and certainly will not lack the desideratum of fresh air.' *Handbook for Travellers in Derbyshire, Nottinghamshire and Leicestershire* (Murray, 1868)

did at Cheltenham, Malvern, Bath, Brighton and elsewhere.

These towns depended chiefly on the middle classes on holiday, ill or retired, for the upper classes visited each other in the country or went abroad, and the working classes, generally speaking, did not get beyond the range of fairly short day excursions—to Margate from London, for instance, or from industrial Lancashire to Blackpool, but hardly to Bournemouth or Torquay. Nor were they welcome if they came, for the 'better-class' resorts despised the day trippers and, far from encouraging them, did their best to keep them away. They brought little money into the town and they scared away those who brought a good deal. Most resorts, even if their exclusiveness was questionable, looked towards wealth and social consequence, and what they sought to provide, in Escott's words, were 'in their most highly finished shape, the amusements of which polite society is especially fond'.

The promenade at Buxton, Derbyshire, from an engraving after Randolph Caldecott, 1877

(Preceding page)
St Martin's in the Fields. Painting by William Logsdail, 1888

Towns so thoroughly dominated by the middle class as the watering-places and the dormitories were something new in English life. They represented, in its extreme form, the physical separation of classes which the Industrial Revolution had brought about. The ancient towns of England—assize towns, cathedral towns, seaports—were mixed in their population and so small that a man could not live very far from his fellows, whether his social equals or not. But in the new industrial towns the richer people kept as separate as they could for the very good reason, amongst others, that they did not want to catch the diseases of their poorer neighbours. They lived in their own districts or, for preference, moved right away. The condition of the slums on the other side of the town, when revealed to them, they regarded with much the same kind of semi-incredulous horror that was aroused by travellers' tales of savage Africa. Indeed late Victorian social workers' accounts of their experience have very much the same flavour as contemporary records of exploration in a foreign land.

Far at the head of all the towns of England in size, in growth, in mingled magnificence and squalor, and in the immensity of its problems, stood London. People poured in from the nearer counties, from the farther counties, from Scotland and Ireland, from beyond the seas. Whereas other large towns, for the most part, got their people fairly locally, London attracted them from all parts. The Census of 1881 showed as many as sixteen per thousand Londoners foreign-born, and that was before the great Jewish arrivals.

Already at the first Census, in 1801, London had had nearly eleven per cent of the total population of England and Wales, and after that for ninety years or so its population grew faster than the population of the country as a whole. By the time the 1901 Census was taken there were $4\frac{1}{2}$ million Londoners, just under fourteen per cent of all the people in England and Wales. These figures, however, are very inexact, for it is impossible to give a single definition of 'London'. To the police it meant one area, to the Registrar-General another, to the London County Council (when in 1888 it was set up) yet another, and so on. For the houses, the streets and the shops pushed outwards all the time, ever further into the surrounding counties, so that it became more and more difficult to say where London ended. The same sort of thing was happening round the great provincial towns, but nowhere on anything like so vast a scale.

The Victorians, speaking generally, did not love towns;

Houndsditch in 1872, from an engraving after Gustave Doré. 'Throughout this neighbourhood —that is, in the open—there is a valiant cheeriness full of strength. The humours of the place are rough and coarse—as the performances in the penny gaffs and public house sing-songs testify; but there is everywhere a readiness to laugh. The vendor of old clothes, who addresses the bystanders in Houndsditch, throws jests into his address. Cheap-Jack must be a humourist, let him appear where he may—in England.' Gustave Doré and Blanchard Jerrold, *London, A Pilgrimage,* 1872

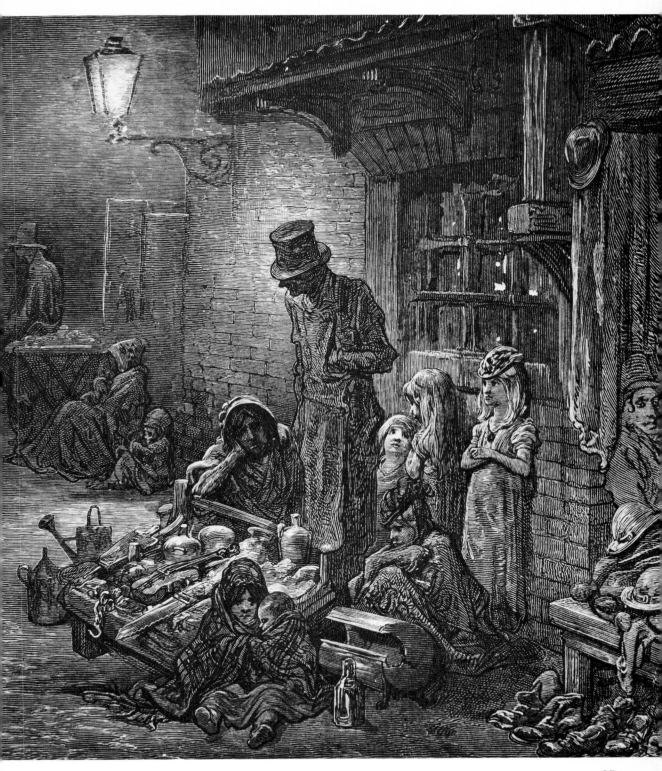

they had a bad conscience about them. London, though, for all its faults, they felt constrained to praise, and they constantly applied the word 'metropolis' to it. 'The metropolis of the Empire', says the Report of the 1871 Census, 'stands . . . by itself; it is the seat of the Legislature, the primary Home of Justice, Medicine, and Religion, the theatre for the fine arts and the sciences, the great centre of society; the emporium of commerce, the warehouse of England, the great Port in communication with the sea. Spanning the broad tidal waters of the embanked Thames with its magnificent bridges, it wants but a greater number of grand public buildings to be the first Queen of Cities.'

Large towns of the modern kind, with all their vigour, all their horror and all their opportunities, first came into being in Victorian England, and much of their physical structure has lasted into the latter part of the twentieth century. In the growing towns, turbulent and squalid like Widnes, decorous and respectable like Eastbourne, or in London itself which in a sense comprehended them all, most of Queen Victoria's English subjects spent most of their lives. They were cut off from the ways of their forefathers; they shaped the ways of their descendants. It is their life—the life of the townspeople of England—which will principally be described in the remaining chapters of this book.

An Irish crossing-sweeper, from an engraving of 1861 after an early photograph. With horse transport, streets were extremely dirty; hence the crossing-sweeper to clear the way, especially for women with long skirts

5 Town life: the Poor

The barbarous poverty of the industrial towns was not the Victorians' fault. The worst of it they inherited. It shamed them and they did their best to put it right, but they were tackling the emergence of a new social order and they had no precedents to guide them. Moreover, there was a good deal in the orthodox Victorian outlook which was a positive hindrance. If you insisted on seeing most problems in moral terms and if, on the whole, you believed that virtue was rewarded and vice punished, then it was easy to blame the poor for their own misfortunes, which they could put right by sobriety, industry and devotion to their masters' interests. Hence the misdirection of much well-meant effort into charity for the 'deserving poor'. If, on top of all that, you believed that it was no business of the State to interfere between master and man, or to tax one section of the community for the benefit of another, or, in general, to do anything more than keep the peace and protect property, then clearly you could not accept the idea of massive State action to relieve poverty. And a radical assault on the problem of poverty, as later generations have discovered, needed State action on a scale to horrify almost all sections of nineteenth-century opinion, let alone the most orthodox. In any case, the good Bible-reading Christian was inclined to take a rather fatalistic view of the whole affair. Had it not been said, on the highest authority, 'the poor ye have always with you'?

By the middle of Queen Victoria's reign there seemed to be fairly good grounds for believing that the economic system would in the long run get rid of poverty automatically, without very much more than a shove here and a prod there from a Parliament elected on a democratic franchise. For anyone could see, and if he could not see there were plenty of statistics to tell him, that more working-class people than ever before were able to live in something like comfort, and that their number was increasing. This was true, and the truth of it is explored in greater detail in the next chapter. At the same time it was also true that the comfortable working class had only recently emerged in any considerable numbers, that only a thin line divided them from poverty, and that old age, sickness, trade depression or some other quirk of fortune might at any time push the individual and his family back into it again. Poverty lay at the root of working-class life and had a powerful influence on the ways of life and habits of thought of the whole new race of town-bred working men. Even when they found themselves more or less securely above the line of want, they did not easily shake off a dread of falling back into the slough they had climbed out of. It is that slough which we are about to explore.

Quite how many people were very badly off it is impossible to say precisely. There were a great many more, proportionately, in the forties than in the eighties, but the population grew so fast that in absolute figures there were probably more people in poverty at the end of the Queen's reign than at the beginning. Charles Booth, in the nineties, thought that about one-third of the population might then have been in poverty, with an income of 21s. (£1.05) or 22s. (£1.10) a week for a small family or 25s. (£1.25) or 26s. (£1.30) for a large one. People at this level, as he put it, might not be in actual want, but 'would be better for more of everything'. Not far below this level 'actual want' would presumably set in, and it has to be borne in mind that in the nineties the population of England and Wales was some thirty million people, so that we are dealing with figures of the order of ten million or so. Sir Robert Giffen, who was not a pessimist in these matters, calculated that on the basis of figures for 1885 some fifty-nine per cent of grown men earned 25s. (£1.25) or less a week, and he thought the average earnings of all grown men might run to about £60 a year, which would imply a great many getting a good deal less.

Who were 'the poor'? Speaking very broadly it might be said, for a start, that they would include all unskilled men without a regular trade. There were poor tradesmen as well, particularly in trades that were being killed by the factories, such as hand-loom weaving, but in general a man with a trade had 'a living in his hands' and some security against destitution. Not so the docker, the factory 'hand', the general labourer, or the labourers working for craftsmen such as bricklayers, for ever on the edge of a trade without a hope of getting into it. Then there were those who lived by all those unorganized, casual employments which Henry Mayhew investigated so thoroughly in London in the middle of the century, and whom he called 'all that large class who live by either selling, showing, or doing something through the country'. In London itself he distinguished six 'distinct genera' of street-folk—street-sellers, street-buyers, street-finders, street-performers, street-artisans or working pedlars and street-labourers—and each of these again he divided minutely. They had one thing in common—their poverty—which forced them to find a living in the most unlikely and

Chimney sweep, Greenwich, 1884

unprofitable ways, and they shaded off by imperceptible and (by themselves) unperceived degrees from honesty into crime, for it was from amongst the very poor that the overwhelming majority of the inhabitants of the prisons came. And some of the worst Victorian poverty was amongst the immigrant Irish, who came in right at the bottom of the labour market to jobs which not even the poorest English, if they could help it, would take on.

No skill could protect a man from sickness, old age or premature death. Any of these could bring a workman or his widow and children to poverty, and they often did. The proper thing to do, of course, was to save in prosperity against the day of adversity, but even the wages of a skilled man in full work allowed little enough margin, and not even the most grinding thrift could meet the strain of chronic illness, of bringing up fatherless children, of prolonged senility. A benevolent employer might come to the help of an old servant. There might be local charities, if an old man, an old woman or an orphan child could get a nomination. There were institutions like the training ship *Exmouth*, Dr Barnardo's Homes, and the Waifs' and Strays' Society which struggled with the flood of neglected children. But in general those who could not look after themselves, from whatever cause, formed a great part of 'the poor' and they had small hope of rescue except into the workhouse.

'What security has the working man?' asked Engels in 1844. 'He knows that, though he may have the means of living today, it is very uncertain whether he shall to-morrow.' Great numbers, certainly, were unemployed or under-employed, though the numbers varied with the state of trade and it is impossible to get accurate figures. Sir John Clapham suggested that they might run from 4 per cent of the working population in a good year like 1850 to 9·5 per cent in a bad year like 1886. In particular occupations the figures might from time to time run much higher. Clapham quotes trade union figures for ironfounders, for blacksmiths, and for boilermakers and iron shipbuilders, in the bad year 1886, which go from 13·9 per cent to 22·2 per cent, and if so many skilled craftsmen were out of work it is almost certain that unskilled men were much worse off—hence the Pall Mall riots in the autumn of that year. And the kind of crisis

Free breakfast in Whitecross Street, London, 1878. '£5 will pay for the charity of a wholesome meal to 400 destitute people, and fifty may be fed once for 12s 6d [62½p] . . . Religious exhortations, with prayers and hymns, accompany or follow these repasts.' (*The Illustrated London News*, 5th January 1878)

100

101

which could produce unemployment on a large scale—something which no workman, however prudent, could do much to protect himself against—happened quite frequently; so much so that the trade cycle was accepted as a law of nature. If depression was prolonged, it was one of the main causes of poverty. The industries of Wednesbury were depressed from the mid-seventies right up to 1914 and the workhouse in that town got so full, from time to time, that paupers had to be boarded out. Some were said to have died of starvation. In 1879 the Local Board took on thirty-five men out of sixty applicants to break stone at 2*s*. 6*d*. (12½p) a cubic yard. In a month they had six months' supply. Sometimes a soup kitchen would be opened by public subscription (Mrs Beeton in her early editions included recipes for soup for the poor at a cost of about 4*d*. (about 1½p) a gallon). Sometimes boots would be given to poor children who could not otherwise go to school. Sometimes meals would be distributed to the aged.

Apart from total unemployment, under-employment was always a risk, particularly to outworkers and small masters who might often suffer from it even when employment generally was good. For factory hands and miners it might take the form of short-time working, so that what was just

Unemployment relief in London's East End. 'The Mansion House Fund, up to last Tuesday, amounted to £75,000, of which only £800 remained for distribution. Among the latest contributions was one of £82 subscribed by the workmen of the Great Eastern Railway Company's locomotive and carriage factory at Stratford. The scene in front of one of the district offices for distributing relief tickets is shown . . .' (*The Illustrated London News*, 27th March 1886)

about a living wage on full time would fall short. Many jobs, especially unskilled ones, were seasonal and could never bring in regular money. Many men, in fact, can never have known what steady employment was. They would spend long hours idly about the street, and one of Charles Booth's collaborators of the nineties gives a telling description: 'A noticeable thing in poor streets is the mark left on the exterior of the houses. All along the front, about on a level with the hips, there is a broad dirty mark, showing where the men and lads are in the constant habit of standing, leaning a bit forward, as they smoke their pipes, and watch whatever may be going on in the street, while above and below the mortar is picked or kicked from between the bricks.' Many of the Victorian poor were people who had no hope of ever doing more than picking up a few days' or a few weeks' money here and there, existing in the intervals as best they could, like the London dockers. And so they jolted down an uneven road of poverty to old age in the workhouse, if they lived so long.

The life of the poor, and of the working class as a whole, was ruled by the factories. Not that everybody worked in them—far from it—but the livelihood of a great many who did not—railwaymen, miners, dockers, for example—depended on their prosperity. Moreover, the factory was symbolic of the whole industrial way of life, with its regular hours and its machine-made discipline. These in particular the workman in the early days of factory industry found hard to get used to. In the fields work altered with the seasons. In cottage industry work might be even harder and more grinding than in a factory, but if a man had put together a little money he could get drunk for a few days and forget it all, and much the same applied to the work of hand craftsmen. In a factory none of this was possible. The work was hard, regular, monotonous. 'Steadiness' was all, as the employers tried to impress upon their hands, and 'steadiness' was not a natural characteristic of the lower-class Englishman. But necessity drove, and he got used to it.

Factories were of all kinds, large, small, good, bad. There were large ironworks like the Cyfarthfa works outside Merthyr Tydfil. There were engineering works like Peter Fairbairn's at Leeds, where in the forties 500 to 600 men were employed—a very large number for those days. There were small masters' shops with a handful of men in the metal trades of Birmingham and Sheffield. There were the Staffordshire potteries, the Lancashire cotton mills.

Over so wide a range and over so long a period as sixty years it is risky to generalize about factory conditions, particularly since the idea was gaining ground all the time that it might, after all, be the business of the State to see that something like decent standards of working safety and welfare were observed. But it is probably safe to say that usually the smaller a factory and the less organized the labour, the worse conditions would be. Also there was a tendency to legislate for particular industries rather than for factory industry as a whole, so that abuses which were checked in the cotton industry in the forties—or something very like them—might still be going on in, say, the Potteries in the sixties. And right at the end of the century there were things going on in match factories and sweatshops in the East End of London which had long been stamped out of larger establishments more closely watched, where the power of factory legislation could be brought to bear.

The archetype of all Victorian factories was the Lancashire cotton mill, although by the middle of the century it was losing its pre-eminence. It would be a many-windowed building several storeys high, such as the one described by Taine, a French observer of the early sixties, which had six storeys and forty windows on each floor. Gas lighting would heat and foul the atmosphere, and the noise of steam-driven looms was described in 1843 as '. . . so stunning and confounding, that a stranger finds it almost utterly impossible to hear a person speak to him . . . or even to hear himself speak'. But the best of the cotton mills represented the highest standards of their time in factory building. Considerate owners would pay attention to such matters as proper ventilation and would show off the results with pride. The worst horrors were in much smaller places, often not built for industrial purposes at all, such as the London match factory of the early sixties which was called 'a wretched place, the entrance to which is through a perfectly dark room, much like a cowhouse'.

The trouble was that many employers were not men of much substance, being often only a few degrees better off than the people who worked for them. They had capital only for the immediate necessities of production and little to spare for amenities even if they had a mind to provide them. This might not have mattered so much if they had only been concerned with the factory itself; but too often they, or men of like mind and similarly scant resources, put up houses too.

Some employers did the job conscientiously and well. In

104

A match factory in the East End, from an engraving. In 1888 the girls of Bryant & May's match factory in London, with help from Annie Besant and other Fabians, struck, gained immense public support, and forced the firm to improve wages and conditions; one of the first important strikes by unskilled workers

1854 James Wilson, one of the owners of Price's Patent Candle Company, built a village alongside his new works on the Cheshire bank of the Mersey which combined decent cottages with space and light. About the same time a much larger scheme was set going in Yorkshire. Sir Titus Salt, a Bradford mill-owner, decided in 1850 to move his works to open country near Shipley, on the River Aire. He built a very large mill, opened in 1853, and round about it laid out Saltaire. In 1854, 150 houses were ready, and by the time Sir Titus died in 1876 there were over 800, each with parlour and kitchen, two or three bedrooms and a backyard. There was a school, too, and an 'institute'; a Congregational church in a startling Italianate style of architecture and a park on the river bank. Much later in the century W. H. Lever at Port Sunlight, Cadbury's at Bourneville, and others followed the example set by such men as Wilson and Salt. All this was excellent, but too commonly 'the prevailing consideration', in the words of a witness before the Poor Law Commissioners about 1840, 'was not how to promote the health and comfort of the occupants, but how many cottages could be built upon the smallest space of ground and at the least possible cost'.

Town life cannot be healthy without sanitation. In over-

Drawing water from a stand-pipe in Fryingpan Alley in Clerkenwell. The stand-pipe, which served the whole neighbourhood, was turned on for 20 minutes a day. From an engraving of 1864

crowded courts, alleys and back streets there was practically none. Privies were usually insufficient and were shared between households, and adequate drainage came slowly and late. Filthy conditions persisted and the Royal Commission on Housing, in the eighties, produced a report which reads quite as disgustingly as anything Chadwick had written forty or more years before. Of one London parish the Commissioners said: 'It seems to be no uncommon thing for the closets to be stopped and overflowing for months', and again: 'in some parts of London they are used as sleeping places by the houseless poor. . . . In Bristol privies actually exist in living rooms: and elsewhere in the provinces there are instances where no closet accommodation at all is attached to the dwellings of the labouring classes.' To the household refuse and human filth there was often added the filth of animals, for many families, following in less suitable surroundings the old cottagers' tradition, kept pigs or fowls in the backyard.

Water supplies were as bad as sanitation. The mains ran usually under the principal streets so that households in the poorer districts had to depend on water from tanks or stand-pipes some way off. A man living in Bath about 1840 could get no good water nearer than a quarter of a mile. 'It is as valuable as strong beer', he said. 'We can't use it for cooking, or anything of that sort, but only for drinking and tea.' 'Then where do you get water for cooking and washing?' 'Why, from the river. But it is muddy, and often stinks bad, because all the filth is carried there.' 'Do you then prefer to cook your victuals in water which is muddy and stinks to walking a quarter of a mile to fetch it from the pump?' 'We can't help ourselves, you know. We couldn't go all that way for it.'

If people would not 'go all that way' for water to cook with, how much less willingly would they fetch water for washing, especially in the dark of a winter morning before they went to the mill or after they came back, twelve, fourteen or sixteen hours later, or in rain, sleet or snow. 'The minor comforts of cleanliness', wrote Edwin Chadwick in 1842—and what he said would have held true much later—'are of course foregone, to avoid the immediate and greater discomforts of having to fetch water.' A Lancashire collier, about the same date, said he never washed his body; he let his shirt rub the dirt off, though he added, 'I wash my neck and ears and face, of course.' The sense of smell was stunned, and observers remarked how little the working class seemed

to be discommoded by the mixture of stenches in which they had to live.

In the lower depths of Victorian towns anything like good housekeeping was impossible. The houses, to start with, were much too full. With large families, with houses divided between households, it was not uncommon to find seven or eight people sleeping in one room, and many families had only two or three rooms or fewer for all purposes. Then dirt would drop from the soot-laden sky and be carried in on people, and all the while there would be far too little money.

Not that many of the women had much idea what good housekeeping was. They had not been in service in good households like country girls. Instead they had mostly been trying to earn a few pence to help their parents' struggles, so that they had had no chance to learn how to be a house-wife even if there had been anyone to teach them. In particular their extravagance in buying and using food was

Census enumerator in a London slum, from *The Illustrated Times*, 7th April 1861. Writing towards the end of the century, Charles Booth commented: 'It appears that, tested by the crowded conditions in which they live, street-sellers, coal-porters and dock-labourers are the poorest sections of the population.' 69 per cent of street-sellers' families lived two or more people to a room; 65 per cent of coal-porters' families; 63 per cent of dock-labourers' families

often deplored by middle-class commentators. They admitted, however, that it was to some extent unavoidable because the working-class woman, living from day to day on a tiny uncertain income, had to buy in very small quantities from hucksters as poor as or poorer than herself. They sought to protect themselves against bad debts by outrageous prices for inferior and adulterated goods.

Nevertheless it was possible, as long as the money was coming in, to feed a family quite well even before the age of cheap imported food. It was said that the working men of Birmingham in the forties could generally contrive a good Sunday joint and on other days steak or chops—'which', as a middle-class observer commented, 'is the most improvident mode either of purchasing or cooking meat'.

Whether the generality of working people in the forties did as well as these meat-eaters of Birmingham seems doubtful. In Manchester a little later, mill hands and their families were said to be living mostly on bad tea, oatmeal and potatoes, with meat (including bacon) not more than three times a week at the most. Something very similar was reported by Charles Booth, in the nineties, as the diet of the poorest in London, though by then margarine and jam were both mentioned as well as bread. Low but regular wages— presumably the same sort of income as that of the mill hand in the fifties—would by the nineties provide a much better living. 'A good deal of bread is eaten and tea drunk', says Booth, 'especially by the women and children, but . . . bacon, eggs and fish appear regularly in the budgets. A piece of meat cooked on Sunday serves also for dinner on Monday and Tuesday, and puddings . . . are regular . . . , not every day, but sometimes in the week.' 'On the whole', Booth concludes, 'these people have enough, and very seldom too much, to eat; and healthy though rather restricted lives are led.'

Booth's opinion must be treated with respect, but in the poorer quarters of Victorian towns it must have been extremely difficult to lead anything like a 'healthy life' as the phrase is understood today. The great spectacular outbreaks of cholera were brought under control, though not before the eighties, but there were plenty of other epidemic diseases, and at all times bad water supplies, filth and overcrowding might produce typhoid, typhus and 'fever' generally, besides tuberculosis, diphtheria and other infectious maladies. Then there were rickets and other diseases of malnutrition, and in general the stunted physique and pale faces of the town poor were continually remarked on throughout the century. Things were certainly better when Booth wrote than they had been, but in the poorer districts there might still have been a good deal of truth in Southwood Smith's words, written in 1844: 'The poorer classes . . . are exposed to causes of disease and death which are peculiar to them; the operation of these peculiar causes is steady, unceasing, sure; and the result is the same as if twenty or thirty thousand of these people were annually taken out of their wretched dwellings and put to death, the actual fact being that they are allowed to remain in them and die.'

Poverty bore much harder on the women than on the men, who had no inducement to stay in their houses longer than they needed for eating and sleeping, and every temptation to get out of them. 'The moral influence of filth and discomfort has never been sufficiently attended to', wrote Southwood Smith in 1844. 'The wretched state of his home is one of the most powerful causes which induce a man to spend his money on strictly selfish gratifications: he comes home tired and exhausted; he wants quiet; he needs re-

Public vaccination in the East End, from an engraving after E. Buckman, 1871. In 1871, according to the Census Report, a 'severe epidemic of small-pox' killed over 23,000 people in England and Wales

The Black Country round Wolverhampton, 1866. 'The lurid smoke and flame of the countless furnaces and forges, with the fire of many heaps of burning refuse thrown up at the mouths of the pits, fill the sky with a fierce glare, which throws out in gigantic shadow the shapes of the buildings, tall chimneys and machines, or of passing workmen, carts and horses, railway-trains, and barges on the canals, rendering the scene one of the strangest and most fantastic that can be witnessed anywhere.' (*The Illustrated London News*, 8th December 1866)

freshment: filth, squalor, discomfort in every shape, are around him; he naturally gets away from it if he can.' And about fifty years later the vicar of a City parish observed: 'The men have a good time compared to the women, who lead fearfully hard and slavish lives.' A decent man in the nineties, earning 25s. (£1.25) a week, might give his wife 20s. (£1.00). On that, in the words of a nurse who knew the London poor, 'she ought to be able to, because in many cases she does, feed four children, dress them and herself, and pay rent.'

The 'strictly selfish gratifications' mentioned by South-wood Smith are more outspokenly described by Engels. 'Next to intemperance in the enjoyment of intoxicating liquors', he wrote, 'one of the principal faults of English working-men is sexual license.' In this last matter later

111

commentators, if they deal with it at all, generally agree with Engels that the poor (though emphatically not the 'respectable' working class) had a very hazy idea of the marriage bond and took their pleasures as they could. Escott, as late as the eighties, reported that workmen in the Black Country had exchanged wives on their way home from the pub, 'and their neighbours have not been shocked'. As to drink, which was much more openly discussed, temperance reformers' minds were much exercised over the question whether the poor were wretched because they drank or whether they drank because they were wretched. The first was the orthodox view and the enthusiastic tee-totaller could usually find, to prove his point, some re-formed drunkard living in frugal comfort on the money which he said he had formerly spent on drink. But a lot of people who knew the poor well, from Southwood Smith to Booth, were more or less unwillingly compelled to the belief that the poor man was a victim of his circumstances to a much greater degree than the moralist would allow.

The pub played a great part in the life of the poor. In it, before the Saturday half-holiday became general in the latter part of the century, wages would be paid on a Satur-day night, so that a good deal of money never went to the households it was supposed to support. In it friendly societies, burial clubs, trade unions would have their head-quarters. Outside it, as the teetotallers pointed out, wives and children would wait while father drank the week's wages within (but it was not unknown for mother to help him do so). Altogether, as the High Church rector of a Norfolk town observed in 1863, 'the poor man goes to the public-house as the rich to his club, more that he may enjoy society than drink.' But Mr Armstrong was unusually tolerant; he would hardly have found many of his brother clergy to agree with him.

The upbringing of children in the households of the poor was bound to be a sketchy affair. Father would be working probably twelve hours a day or more if he was fully em-ployed, and if he was not it was unlikely that he would take much responsibility for what he would regard as his wife's job. Mother herself, if she could, would almost certainly try to get some kind of paid work to help out the tiny household income. If she did that, she too would probably be out of the house most of the day (though she might get one of the miserably paid domestic occupations like sewing or match-box making). The smaller children would have to be looked

The schoolroom of a Boys' Home, from an engraving in the *Illustrated London News*, 1870. 'It is about twelve years since a few earnest men established the Boys' Home, to receive destitute children in danger of falling into a criminal life . . . The boys are taught habits of order, cleanliness and industry. The average cost of maintenance for each boy is £15 1s 2d [just under £15.07] . . . the average net cost in the reformatories of Great Britain is £18 19s 3d [about £18.95], and that of London pauper children never less than £24 10s [£24.50].' (*The Illustrated London News,* 2nd April 1870)

after by the larger, of their own or another family, though in later years the new Board schools provided a useful child-minding service, and a Baptist minister said in the nineties that London washerwomen would send their children to school in the mornings and then be out themselves until eight or nine in the evenings. Children not at school—or at work—spent their time in the streets, but infants too small for that were too often drugged with 'Godfrey's Cordial' or some other concoction of opium and treacle. By these preparations, as the report on the state of large towns put it in 1844, 'great numbers of infants perish, either suddenly, from an overdose, or, as more commonly happens, slowly, painfully, and insidiously.' Great numbers of infants perished anyhow, whether from that cause or some other, and their death cannot always have been unwelcome.

Both boys and girls went young to work, because of the overwhelming necessity to get every possible penny into the household. Until the State took matters seriously in hand from 1870 onward, schooling was likely to be sketchy in the extreme, for among the poor those parents would be altogether exceptional who would not grudge the time and the few pence a week that would have to be spent on it. As late

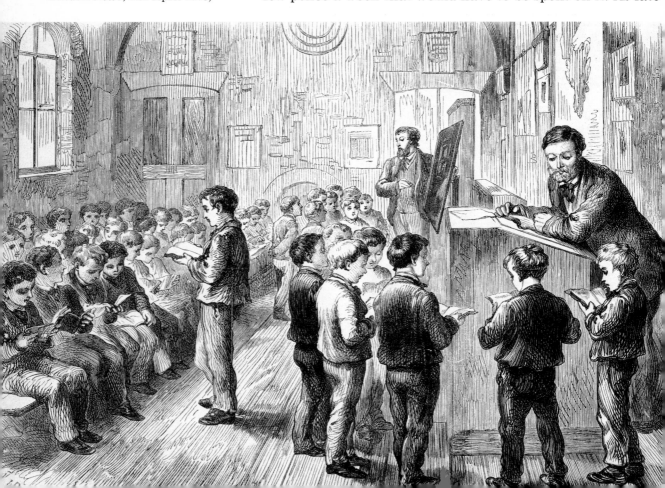

as 1880, according to the Census Report of 1881, something like twenty per cent of the population could not sign their names, and in 1850 the figure had been forty per cent. Only about half the children aged five to fifteen were then at school.

The employment of children in the textile industries and in the mines was regulated by law during the forties, after shocking revelations by the Children's Employment Commission, and the regulations were enforced by inspection. But there were still plenty of trades unregulated altogether and another Children's Employment Commission, sitting in the sixties, found, for instance, 11,000 children and young persons in the Potteries employed 'under conditions which undermine their health and constitution'. What that meant, amongst other things, was that small boys between six and ten years old were carrying moulds from the potters to the 'stoves' (small rooms at a temperature of 120 degrees or so) for about $11\frac{1}{2}$ hours a day nominally, but in fact for as much as 14, 15 or 16 hours, and they were getting perhaps as much as half a crown ($12\frac{1}{2}$p) a week for it. Other trades that were investigated were lucifer match-making, with its hideous possibilities of jaw disease caused by phosphorus, paper staining and chimney sweeping.

Children in the mines, from the Report of the Royal Commission of 1842.

As to the last, there had been a great scandal about climbing chimney sweeps in the thirties, and in the middle of Queen Victoria's reign the comfortable classes were inclined to think that matters had been put right by an Act of 1840. On the contrary, the Commissioners of the sixties reported that 'the evil is decidedly on the increase'. The job meant climbing up long, twisting, soot-covered flues, and the brutality required to get a boy to do it was sickening. 'No one', said a Nottingham master sweep called Ruff, 'knows the cruelty which a boy has to undergo in learning. The flesh must be hardened. This is done by rubbing it, chiefly on the elbows and knees, with the strongest brine, close by a hot fire. You must stand over them with a cane, or coax them with the promise of a halfpenny, &c., if they will stand a few more rubs. At first they will come back from their work with their arms and knees streaming with blood, and the knees looking as if the caps had been pulled off; then they must be rubbed with brine again.'

Probably the worst exploitation of child labour did not happen where the children were directly employed by the owners of large, or fairly large, businesses. Conditions were hardest where the children worked for craftsmen employed at piece work rates, as for instance in the Potteries and in hand block printing for wallpaper. These men still had the old, irregular habits of work that had been common before the factories enforced regular attendance between stated hours. A potter would take two or three days off, if he felt inclined and could afford it, and then work excessively hard to make up for it—hence, to some extent, the fifteen or sixteen hours which his attendant jigger turners and mould runners intermittently had to work.

Worst of all, perhaps, were parents employing their own children in their own homes. A girl speaking of glove-making said that her 5½-year-old sister, after two years' experience, could stitch very well, and she went on: 'Little children are kept up shamefully late, if there is work, especially on Thursday and Friday nights, when it is often till 11 or 12. They have to make two days out of Friday. Mothers will pin them to their knee to keep them to their work, and, if they are sleepy, give them a slap on the head to keep them awake. If the children are pinned up so, they cannot fall when they are slapped or when they go to sleep. . . . The child has so many fingers set for it to stitch before it goes to bed, and must do them.'

This was the harsh world of the Victorian poor bearing down on those who, above all, were least able to protect themselves. It is fair to add that the fact was recognized. The Commission's reports were followed by legislation and some of the scandals were suppressed.

This account of the Victorian poor, grim though it may be thought, has not yet touched the very bottom of the social system. Mayhew, in the fifties, found people in London who

The sewer-hunter, from an engraving of 1861. 'There were known to be a few years ago nearly 200 sewer-hunters, or 'toshers', and, incredible as it may appear, I have satisfied myself that, taking one week with another, they could not be said to make much short of £2 per week . . . With their gains, superior even to those of the better-paid artisans, and far beyond the amount received by many clerks . . . the shore-men might, with but ordinary prudence, live well, have comfortable homes, and even be able to save sufficient to provide for themselves in their old age.' (Henry Mayhew, 1851). The sewerage system of London was reconstructed in the early sixties and 'this splendid system of main drainage' was opened by the Prince of Wales in 1865

made a living by searching the sewers for what they could find, and others who collected dogs' droppings to sell to tanneries. Quintin Hogg, starting a ragged school in 1865, found one or two boys sent to him with no clothes but their mothers' shawls pinned round them. In 1885 the Prince of Wales, Cardinal Manning and the other members of the

Royal Commission on Housing heard of people who crowded the stairs and passages of East End tenement houses at night, and who were known as ''appy dossers'. Charles Booth, later again, wrote of '. . . the lowest class . . . which cannot be associated in any regular way with industrial or family life . . . the common lodging-house caters for their necessities and the public-house for their superfluities. Their ultimate standard of life is almost savage, both in its simplicity and in its excesses.'

With such as these this chapter has not tried to deal in detail. It has simply tried to indicate, broadly, the sort of conditions under which many people in the new industrial towns, and these not the very poorest, had to live. It has to be borne in mind that life for the working man had always

A London lodging-house, from an engraving of 1872

been hard, often wretched, and nineteenth-century wretchedness may not have been so bad as that of former centuries. At any rate, it attracted much more attention and much more was done about it. But it remains true that it made for a brutal, barbarous existence which was the despair of the middle-class moralist and the dread of the 'comfortable' working class who had raised themselves above it.

It was a world which the accepted Victorian scale of values and ideas of right behaviour hardly penetrated. Thrift meant nothing to people so poor that they could live only for the day. 'Self-help' and individual ambition were alike a mockery to people so weighed down by circumstances over which they had no control. How could conventional morality make any sense to people sleeping seven or eight to a room? In fact, there was a good deal of prostitution, the marriage bond was fairly loose, and illegitimate children were easily accepted into their mothers' families. Of religious belief, except of the vaguest kind, there was practically none except among the Catholic Irish, the Jews and occasional pockets of far-out nonconformity. The law was a doubtful protection, the property of the rich a more or less legitimate target, and the police potential oppressors. In any case, life in gaol might be more comfortable and would certainly be healthier than life outside.

So far as the poor man felt himself to have any friends, they were of his own kind and his strength lay in united action with them, though the unskilled labourers only slowly recognized how great that united strength might be. But commentators from Engels in the forties to Charles Booth half a century later remarked on the helpfulness of the poor to each other, in spite of the general brutality of their way of life and of much of their conduct. 'It is only the poor that really give', said a nonconformist minister to one of Booth's investigators. 'Personal help and timely relief are the key notes of the charity of the poor. They know exactly the wants of one another and give when needed.' So much for the brisk and tight-lipped charity of the middle classes, seeking always to distinguish the 'deserving poor' from the rest. And a Catholic priest agreed with the nonconformist. 'To each other', he said, 'their goodness is wonderful.'

6 Town life: the comfortable working classes

A policeman, from an engraving after Phil May, 1895

Ten shillings (50p) a week, in Charles Booth's opinion, could bridge the gap between poverty and comfort. He thought there might be one-third of the population 'who have . . . taking the year round, from 25*s*. [£1.25] to 35*s*. [£1.75] a week, among whom would be counted, in addition to wage earners, many retail traders and small masters'. These people would 'enjoy solid working-class comfort'. He draws a very thin line, or rather no line at all, between wage earners and those who employed themselves and, often, others as well. This shows the complexity of the social structure and the danger of assuming identity of interest and outlook amongst members of 'the working class'. In fact squabbles and snobberies within the working class, better described as 'the working classes', were quite as bitter and ran quite as deep as conflicts between Capital and Labour, which were more openly acknowledged. Certainly the great majority of 'respectable working men' would have hastened to dissociate themselves from 'the poor', even though from higher up the social scale they might seem to merge into one indeterminate mass.

The group Booth wrote of would include the skilled workmen—'artisans' was the favourite Victorian word—who were the backbone of the unions: such men as the masons and carpenters in building; the engineers, ironfounders and boilermakers in the metal industries; the compositors in printing; and many more, scattered in key positions and often in small numbers throughout manufacturing industry, mining and transport. Many men of this kind, even though they worked for an employer, were themselves employers rather than wage-earners, for they contracted to do a job and then took on help on their own responsibility. Such was the system among journeymen potters, amongst 'puddlers' in the ironworks, in certain occupations in the textile trades and in coal-mining, and elsewhere. It was a system that had been stronger than it was when Booth wrote, but it still flourished sufficiently to confuse the straight issue between 'employers' and 'employed' and to blur the edges of the social classes.

The comfort which people of this kind were beginning to enjoy, in the latter part of Queen Victoria's reign, depended on a combination of mass-production, cheap fast transport, and the new techniques of mass-marketing which were being exploited by manufacturers like W. H. Lever and distributors like Thomas Lipton. Goods of many kinds were coming into the shops in quantities much greater and at prices much lower than ever before, and earnings were improving. Sir Robert Giffen said that prices rose from about 1842 to about 1872, but wages rose also. After that—he was speaking of the mid-nineties—wages did not rise much but prices fell a lot, especially of food and clothing.

The rise in wages was largely a matter of old low-paid jobs giving place to new, so that by sticking to one old-established trade a man would not necessarily better himself. He might find himself worse off or without a trade at all. But the new society was creating many new occupations, and anyone who got into one of those might do very well for himself. There was the railway service, for instance, and the police, both much prized for security. In 1851 there were about 25,000 railwaymen, taking account only of the more skilled, and fifty years later there were nearly 277,000 (the Census Report for 1901 observes rather acidly that the numbers had risen forty-eight per cent in ten years but 'there was an increase of eight per cent only in the length of line open'). As to the police, there were nearly 45,000 policemen in 1901 and their numbers had been growing for seventy years.

The number of jobs in the old-established textile industries was, if anything, falling, and the same was happening in the clothing trades, where machinery was coming more and more into use. Against that, more and more people were

In the 'sixties and 'seventies, in response to rising demand from the affluent classes, 'department stores' were growing up, which supplied a very large range of goods and services. Some, notably the Civil Service Stores (1865) and the Army and Navy Stores (1871) were co-operatives; others, such as Harrods and Whiteleys, which were growing at about the same time, were privately owned. The shop illustrated seems to be an early example of the type

making machinery (161,000 people in 1871, 342,000 in 1891) and many new or newish industries were growing fast. The 1871 Census Report, for instance, spoke of the rapid growth of the 'india-rubber and gutta-percha manufacture'; the 1891 Report mentioned ready-made clothing; the 1901 Report showed the rise of the bicycle in an increase over ten years of forty-five per cent in the number of vehicle makers, and for the first time 'motor makers' were reported.

For anyone concerned, as we are, with the rising standard of life of ordinary people there is nothing more significant than the rise in the number of those who got their living from the industries working for the mass market and from the services associated with them. By 1891 there were nearly 600,000 people in the food trades; amongst them, the number of jam and preserve makers had gone up by eighty-two per cent over ten years, and there had been an increase of the order of forty per cent in the numbers of greengrocers, grocers, fishmongers and other traders in food.

At the same time other more or less specialized kinds of shopkeepers were becoming more numerous while the old type of general shopkeeper became scarcer—a process rather like that in Africa at the present day where, likewise, a rising standard of living can support increasing specialization among the traders who supply its needs. To take one example, the number of photographers and photographic dealers rose forty-one per cent between 1871 and 1881 and fifty-nine per cent (to nearly 11,000) in the next ten years.

The rise of professional photography. '"Love, Pride, Revenge"—The group represents a Young Minstrel of humble origin, declaring his Passion to a Lady of Noble Parentage. Her haughty Brother, as may be seen from his menacing attitude, is about to Avenge the Insult offered to his Family!' (*Punch*, 10th October 1857)

The working man and his family, like their social superiors, could afford on great occasions to pose stiffly in their best clothes besides the potted palm.

Because of all this new and growing activity, and at the same time helping to create it, there were many second-generation Victorians who were much better off than their parents. They had more money and their money went further. Many of them were less likely to be out of work, and if they were they might have been able to save something to meet the evil day, or they might belong to a union which would help them to find another job and pay something towards their support and their travelling while they sought it. But unemployment, whether caused by bad trade or a strike, was still a bitter thing, and the fear of it was never far from the steady workman's mind.

In prosperity he was much better dressed than his father or his grandfather. Engels had found the Manchester working classes of the forties dressed almost entirely in cotton. Wool and linen were too dear. 'Shirts', he said, 'are made of bleached or coloured cotton goods; the dresses of the women are chiefly of cotton print goods; and woollen petticoats are rarely to be seen on the washline. The men wear chiefly trousers of fustian or other heavy cotton goods, and jackets or coats of the same.' Some sort of head covering was conventionally required but many who were not among the poorest could not afford to buy anything and they would fold themselves 'a low, square paper cap' of the sort which Tenniel gave the carpenter in *Alice in Wonderland*. And a good deal of clothing was either second-hand or home-made, for the day of cheap factory-made clothing was not yet come.

It came with sewing machines and boot-making machinery. By the seventies machinery was sufficiently widespread in the clothing trades to make an impact on the census returns. It was particularly important in footwear, because shoes and boots cannot be made at home and they were always a great problem in poor families. Mechanization brought the price of clothing and footwear down a great deal and by the nineties Booth said of the comfortable working class: 'clothes necessary for comfort are usually good and suitable; they wear well and are well worn. . . . The working clothes are according to the nature of the work. The holiday garments are as nearly as possible in the fashion of the day. As a rule, none of the clothes are second-hand.' The well-to-do might sneer at 'reach-me-downs' (ready-made garments which the shopman would 'reach

A Manchester operative, 1842, from an engraving in *The Illustrated London News*. The illustration accompanies an account of disturbances in the North in August 1842, when the railway system was used to carry large bodies of troops, sent North to keep order. About 10,000 people were reported to have passed through Stalybridge 'very quietly, with the exception of repeated cries that they would have blood for blood.'

126

down' from his shelf), but they allowed the late Victorian working man and his family to appear respectably dressed, and warmly too.

They would feed well also, and with much greater variety than formerly. 'For dinner', says Booth of 'the class of fully paid labour in regular employ', 'meat and vegetables are demanded every day. Bacon, eggs and fish find their place at other times. Puddings and tarts are not uncommon, and bread ceases to be the staff of life. . . . In this class no one goes short of food.' The English farmer might be ruined by the imported cheap meat and grain, but the English town housewife had good reason to be glad of it.

Whole new industries, as we have seen, were springing up to meet the demand which working-class housewives could increasingly afford to satisfy. Margarine, like ready-made clothing, might be despised by the well-to-do, but from its invention about 1870 onwards it was a very welcome substitute or supplement for butter which cost twice as much. Tinned, potted and preserved goods took the place of fresh produce which town-dwellers had no cheap access to, or provided them with things they had never had before, such as bully beef and tinned sardines. A woman of the nineties wrote that the duties of housekeeping had been lightened in innumerable ways, and she supported her point by mentioning 'bought jams, preserved foods, tinned, bottled, fresh and dried productions of all kinds'. No doubt she had middle-class housekeeping chiefly in mind, but a great many of these goods went into working-class homes as well.

Just as abominable housing was at the root of much of the misery of the poor, so 'solid working-class comfort' could not exist without housing which, by the standards of the day, was good or at least tolerable. Town planning and building regulations, as time went on, made the jerry-builder's life more difficult, and it became hard for him to get away with the kind of cottages that had been run up in the forties and before, though far too many that had already been built remained undemolished and the same might be said of formerly good housing that had tumbled down into low-class tenements.

House-building remained almost entirely a matter of private enterprise, inspired by philanthropy, by ordinary commercial motives or sometimes by a mixture of both. The blocks of 'model dwellings', dating from the early sixties onwards, which still stand in great numbers all over inner London, are a massive monument to the Victorian social

Peabody Model Dwellings, Blackfriars Road, London, designed by H. A. Darbishire, 1871. The development consisted of 16 blocks, comprising 384 dwellings and 640 rooms. Writing about 1888, Octavia Hill observed: 'The dweller in towns . . . must sacrifice much for the privileges he obtains, and he must accept the law of considering his neighbour rather by sacrifice of his individual joy, than by the development of individual varied capacity.'

reformer's faith in the capacity of private effort to put right public ills.

George Peabody, an American merchant living in London, put £150,000, later increased to £500,000, in trust for building 'model dwellings' in 1862, and about the same time Sidney Waterlow, working through the Improved Industrial Dwellings Company, began to show that sanitary housing would pay on an average weekly rental of 2*s*. 1¼*d*. (10½p) a room. Other enterprises followed, more or less public-spirited, more or less devoted to the profit motive. One landlord, in an attempt to defeat the provisions of the Housing of the Working Classes Act, 1885, put up a notice saying that no agreement for letting should be deemed to imply any condition on his part that the premises let should be fit for human habitation, but perhaps he was an oddity.

These model dwellings, like other blocks of flats (the

wealthy were taking to flats at about the same time as the poor), were an attempt to get rid of overcrowding by building upwards rather than lengthways—an attempt which would have seemed quite the natural thing in Edinburgh or Paris, but was strange to London. Built generally of drab stock brick, with steep stairs and iron balcony railings, separated from each other by asphalt courtyards, they present an aspect of gaunt discomfort to the twentieth-century eye, but that is not a fair way to judge them.

'The advantages of living in Buildings', wrote 'a Lady Resident' in her 'Sketch of Life in Buildings', '. . . far outweigh the drawbacks. Cheapness, a higher standard of cleanliness, healthy sanitary arrangements, neighbourly intercourse between children and grown-up people, and, perhaps above all, the impossibility of being overlooked altogether, or flagrantly neglected by relatives in illness or old age, seem to be the great gains; and the chief disadvantage, the lack of privacy and the increased facility for gossip and quarrelling . . . introduces a constant variety of petty interest and personal feeling into the monotony of everyday life.'

What these dwellings were doing, as all good housing must do, was to rescue the working man from the unregulated barbarity of the slums, with its squalor and its own peculiar kind of freedom, and to give him instead the chance of reasonable comfort at the price of restriction of his liberty and respect for his neighbour's convenience. Octavia Hill saw the whole picture and described the implications of developing something like a civilized existence for the working class in large towns: 'Under rules they grow to think natural and reasonable, inspected and disciplined, every inhabitant registered and known, school board laws, sanitary laws, and laws of the landlord or company regularly enforced; every infectious case of illness instantly removed, all disinfecting done at public cost, it is a life of law, regular, a little monotonous, and not developing any great individuality, but consistent with happy home-life, and it promises to be the life of the respectable London working-man . . . One feels that men thus trained may be meek, well-ordered, but will not be original nor all-round trained men. One can only note the danger and watch for any way of obviating it in some degree.'

In their progress from undisciplined, truculent barbarity towards middle-class respectability many working men, not only in London, ran remarkably close to the pattern predicted for them by Octavia Hill. But they did not become flat-dwellers on anything like the scale that she expected. The 'model dwellings' themselves provided, perhaps, for 50,000 people or so, but what the respectable working man really wanted, like his respectable middle-class prototype, was a house of his own. It should have three or four bedrooms upstairs, two rooms downstairs, of which one should be a parlour unused except on Sundays, at funerals and on great occasions generally. It ought to have its scrap of ground back and front so that something could be grown and perhaps some form of livestock kept. A London policeman's backyard of the nineties had, every spring, a brood of young ducklings 'and as they gradually leave the scene they are replaced by pigeons; about a third of the ground is devoted to a permanent staff of cocks and hens, just beyond the reach of a dog whose chain allows him to command another considerable portion of the estate.' And the house and ground, however small, should be carefully fenced or walled away from the intrusion and if possible the sight of all outsiders. The result might be claustrophobic but it ensured privacy: a deeply felt want of people not far removed from the teeming promiscuity of the slums or, on the other hand, still regretful of the comparatively unoverlooked life of a country village.

To meet this demand long rows of houses were put up in all the industrial towns and in London throughout the last thirty years or so of Queen Victoria's reign. There was very little Council housing until much later, and they were virtually all put up for private profit. They were not slum property —far from it. They were cramped, for rooms were small, families large, lodgers frequent, and furniture usually most unsuitable, being copied from pieces intended for much larger spaces. Their outlook would generally be dreary, being nothing but a row of similar houses opposite. But they had proper drains, they had water, they had gas, they were reasonably well built, and a life of self-respect and comfort was perfectly possible in them.

Houses of this sort can be seen at their highest development at Port Sunlight, built by W. H. Lever for his workmen from the late eighties on. Few people understood the English working class better than Lever, and behind the luxuries of layout and architectural design with which he indulged his own taste he made sure that his people got what most of them wanted. He put up two main kinds of cottage. One had a kitchen-living-room and scullery, but no parlour,

Planned Housing, Port Sunlight, looking towards the Art Gallery, from an engraving after T. Raffles Davison, 1916. 'It is pleasant to realise that what has become a problem of such a very serious kind in London after so many years of haphazard and chance, is happily barred out of the horizon in the definitely schemed plan of the garden city or the model village.'

and three bedrooms. The other had a parlour as well as a kitchen and scullery, and four bedrooms. Both types had bathrooms. All the cottages had yards, but none had front gardens of their own. This was something of a grievance to a good many of the tenants, but Lever insisted on keeping the public face of the village in his own hands; its lawns and flower beds were looked after by the Company's gardeners and the householders were forbidden to touch them. Lever's ideas on the proper behaviour of his tenantry were no less strict than Octavia Hill's on that of the inhabitants of model dwellings.

Such a life as Port Sunlight represented—orderly, hardworking, with due respect for constituted authority and proper regard for the comforts of a well-run household—was only possible for people well grounded in habits of self-restraint and educated at least up to passable literacy. It is hardly too much to say that it would have been impossible, on any large scale, without universal elementary education. That became the declared purpose of the State with the passing of the Act of 1870, which legislated for the provision of a school within the reach of every child in the country. It became compulsory in 1880, free in 1891. To carry it into effect, Board Schools (i.e. schools run by local School Boards) began to rise in districts that were not already served by schools of the Church of England and other denominations.

At last, during the seventies and eighties, it became hard for any child in England, even the poorest and worst-neglected, to escape altogether from something approaching a civilizing influence. For many the new system meant much more. It meant that as well as being taught their letters and their figures they were quite powerfully indoctrinated with the values of 'respectable' society. For a very few the rather uninviting gateway of the elementary school might open the road to higher education.

Not that the new Board schools struck contemporary observers as 'uninviting', and indeed although many, especially in London, appear gaunt and barracky to us, others were built with a considerable flourish and without too niggardly a regard for expense. The standard London Board School would have three storeys—boys, girls, infants. A child in the nineties might go at three; at five, it must; at seven, it hatched from an infant into a boy or girl. There might be 300 to 500 in the infant department, with 40, 50 or 60 in a class, and for these infants, said Booth, 'school is a

A new Parish School, Leicester. The old parish school of St Mary's, Leicester, put up at the end of the eighteenth century by the vicar of that day, had become too small and was replaced by this stone neo-Gothic building with four classrooms 'provided with screens; so that they may be divided when required' and gas lighting. (*The Illustrated London News*, 25th September 1869)

A board-school class, from an engraving in *Punch*, 1886. The London Board Schools, about 1890, according to Charles Booth, 'accommodate a little over 443,000 children, and have been erected at a cost of about four and a half millions sterling. Taken as a whole, they may fairly be said to represent the high-water mark of the public conscience in this country in its relation to the education of the children of the people.'

place to be happy and comfortable in, more so, in many cases, than the children are or can be in their wretched homes.'

In rough districts, these schools must have been rough, depressing places. In 1889—a year of 'extreme distress'—some 50,000 children in London schools were officially returned as attending in want of food, and Booth, speaking of underfed children generally, commented: 'Puny, pale-faced, scantily clad and badly shod, these small and feeble folk may be found sitting limp and chill on the school benches in all the poorer parts of London.' But these poor waifs and their slightly better-fed and therefore more boisterous companions were for the first time being taken in hand systematically and 'the turbulence of the streets is subdued into industrious calm. Ragged little *gamins* run quietly in harness, obedient to a look, a gesture of the teacher in command. No matter what door we open we find the school work going smoothly and steadily along. Even the baby regiment in the lowest of the infant classes shows the same aptitude for order, and toddles through the programme with an intentness comic to behold.'

The infants had object-lessons, Swedish drill and action songs; by the time they were seven, if they were to pass into Standard I, they had to read, spell and write simple words, besides being capable of some arithmetic and needlework for the girls or drawing for the boys. For children who failed to pass their standards the school could draw no Government grant—a misconceived system which, until it was abolished in 1891, led to a good deal of useless cramming.

Most children in the nineties would leave before they were thirteen, and in the lower-grade schools only about six per cent of the boys stayed into Standard VI. But in the 'higher-grade' or 'higher elementary schools'—the first attempt at State secondary education—which many school boards set up in the later eighties there would be found the children of ambitious, well-off working-class parents, alongside children of the lower middle classes. 'The great bulk of the children', said Booth, 'are wholesome, bright-looking, well-fed, eager for notice, "smart", and full of life.' He went on to say that the work of these schools (which all pupils had to leave at fourteen) was often 'mechanical' and 'too clerkly', yet it was nevertheless 'in quality, scope, and teaching power, distinctly in advance of what even middle-class parents, a few years ago, could secure for their children in the ordinary private school'. He was left with the impression, in some schools, 'that the less desirable characteristics of the lower middle-class are being grafted on those of the upper working class'.

By the age of twenty or so, at the latest, a young working man would hope to be established in some skilled trade and with a good employer—a railway company, perhaps, or a large brewery, or a firm of standing in his native town. Entry into desirable trades—pattern-making, say, or the composing of type—was very closely watched by the craft unions. They might be tiny in numbers and local in influence or they might be numerous and national, like the Amalgamated Society of Engineers, but they would all try to keep down the number of men admitted to their trades so as to keep pay up and employment secure. And in choosing whom they would admit there was no question of open competition. The best qualification—sometimes the only qualification—

Apprentice in a file-cutting shop, Sheffield, 1866: a very unhealthy occupation. 'The file-cutters' disease is poisoning by lead . . . The file while being cut rests upon a bed of lead, and where many are cutting in the same shop fine particles of lead dust abound . . . The men eat their meals without washing their hands, and often take dinner in the workshop where the files are cut; as though fine lead-dust, handling the lead at each shifting, and licking the fingers were not sufficiently poisonous!' *The Illustrated London News,* 10th March 1866

was to have a father or some other close relation already in the trade. Much the same might be said for getting into a job with a good employer, who would be more likely to look at the son, brother or nephew of one of his own people than at an outsider. Outsiders did from time to time force their way into the closest rings and there were always new occupations coming up in which rings had not had time to form, but nevertheless it was extremely difficult for the boy without connections—the boy, that is, from a really poor home, with an unskilled man for a father—to get a start in life.

The upper ranks of the working class, in fact, went on much the same principles as those applied by the aristocracy to choosing officers for 'good' regiments or attachés for the Diplomatic Service. Nepotism was all, or nearly all. The idea of throwing good opportunities open to all comers and letting the best man win was not born in the working class. It was the conception of the Victorian middle class, jealous of the aristocratic monopoly of patronage in official appointments, and its instrument was the written examination, competitive for the Civil Service, qualifying for the professions (see Chapter 7). No one dreamt of applying to the choosing of, say, a potential compositor the methods that were applied to choosing a potential civil servant or doctor.

The workman being established, marriage would follow. He would reach his highest earning power (unless, much later, he became a foreman) when he passed from a boy's to a man's pay, so that the kind of financial considerations which delayed middle-class marriage did not apply, except in so far as a prudent man might wait until he had saved a little money. Nevertheless the better-off a young man was, the later he would be likely to marry. Perhaps he would not feel quite the same urge to get out of a squalid, overcrowded home as he would if he were really poor. Competent observers, towards the end of the century, thought the age of marriage was rising, partly as a result of 'clubs and wider interests', so that a man might marry about the age of twenty-five, a girl a few years younger. If the girl as well as the man had put some money by, the marriage would start on a reasonably firm foundation, but it is to be hoped that not many workmen carried prudence quite so far as Jacob Holyoake, an early historian of the co-operative movement, suggested. 'Many single women', he said, 'have accumulated property in the store, which becomes a certificate of their conjugal worth, and young men in want of prudent help-meets consider that to consult the books of the store is the best means of directing their selection.'

The respectable working classes regarded marriage much more seriously than the poor, and a fall from virtue in a daughter or a sister would be a terrible thing or at least, in Booth's words, 'a subject that it is polite to ignore'. There is no doubt that even in respectable circles pregnancy often came before marriage rather than after, but that was hardly to be considered a lapse from virtue if marriage did in fact follow, preferably not less than six months before the child was born. 'Most young men', said a doctor, 'are bounced into marriage', but perhaps that was an extreme view.

The skilled man's hours of work grew shorter during the latter half of the century. In the fifties and earlier it is probably not untrue to say that twelve hours was regarded as a normal working day for a grown man and much more was often worked. By the nineties, in the opinion of the Royal Commission on Labour, skilled men's hours, 'though untouched by the Factory Acts, have shown a tendency in recent years to approximate to nine a day or fifty-four a week', and the reduction, of course, had affected the hours of craftsmen's labourers too.

Not that workmen were anxious to cut their hours if it meant a cut in earnings too. Some tradesmen could earn good money by piece work, and they went on working very long hours in order to do so. Blast furnaces in the Cleveland

136

district were worked in twelve-hour shifts and on alternate Sunday, and puddlers and millmen had a similar system. It could have been put on an eight-hour basis, but that would have made awkward hours for the puddlers, and the millmen valued the earnings—up to 20*s.* (£1.00) a day—which the long hours yielded. So the hours stayed long. They were long, too, at the other end of the scale of prosperity, in sweated industries such as cheap clothing and cheap furniture, simply because there was great competition for ill-paid work, so that a great deal of it had to be done to earn a very slender livelihood. Long hours, of course, did not always mean hard work, and as examples the Commission quoted 'fourteen hours of duty as a porter at a station on a country branch line, or twelve hours duty as a seaman . . . on a good steamship in calm weather'.

Although hours of work were still long, the workman by the end of the century had established a recognized right to a Saturday half-holiday as well as the biblically ordained Sunday—something which would have been regarded as quite out of the question by earlier generations of em-

The betting office, engraving after John Leech, 1852

ployers. The Saturday half-holiday, in Clapham's view, arose from a Factory Act of 1850 which enforced it in the textile industries. From them, like much else in factory practice, it spread to other trades. When the workman finished and drew his pay at two on Saturday afternoon, rather than late in the evening, his wife could get her shopping done in reasonable time, leaving the evening free. For the really prosperous it made week-end outings possible. And from 1871 onward, as well as the weekly Saturday afternoons, there were four statutory bank holidays in the year.

The workman's ways of spending his leisure, like much else in the national life, became more civilized as time went on. Farnworth Wakes, near Widnes, which specialized in bull-baiting, bear-baiting and cock-fighting, were suppressed in 1865, partly as a result of prolonged efforts by a local parson, and Widnes Cricket Club was started. Wednesbury Wake went on until 1874; then the Home Office suppressed it on account of immorality, drunkenness and extravagance. The local leader of those who had campaigned for suppression went armed for some time, in fear of his life, and as late as 1889 the Wake was still being celebrated on private ground instead of the streets. In the middle-eighties, too, rat-killing and badger-drawing matches were still going on in Wednesbury. But the fact that efforts were made, with greater or less success, to stop such things is significant. Barbarity was losing ground to the comparatively peaceful attractions of organized games which, from the sixties onwards, began to contain the natural aggressiveness of the male within fairly harmless channels.

Organized games led on to professional games, and in the seventies the watching of professional football began to take its place as the working man's Saturday afternoon amusement. It did not, however, supplant his passion for gambling in which, as in some other things, he resembled the upper classes far more than his employers, who sanctified their gambling instincts into the taking of business risks, and condemned as sinners those who indulged theirs for pleasure. Betting on racehorses was widespread, though hampered by the law, and the working man, where he could, would own a greyhound, especially in the Potteries, near Manchester, and among the miners. In London, according to Booth, there were many gambling clubs—opened, raided, closed and opened again—and he describes one in which

Popular entertainment at the music hall: engraving after Richard Doyle, 1864 there was dancing downstairs and *chemin de fer* upstairs, with about sixty men playing it, artisans and shopkeepers amongst them. There was a tape-machine for racing information and the owner was a former champion lightweight boxer; he had another boxer as manager.

There was a growing feeling against drunkenness, though not against drinking. The more a man could drink, the more his mates would respect him, but he ought not to get visibly drunk. London pubs, by the nineties, were growing respectable. Rowdiness was less common; young men would take young women into them 'which fifty years ago was inadmissable', and the publican, instead of being a decayed prize-fighter, would be, in the words of a policeman, 'well educated, respectable, and a keen man of business, who can keep his own accounts . . . and fully realizes that it is to his interest that the law should be strictly observed in his house'.

Amusement, however, respectable, remained something like a male monopoly, at any rate after marriage, and 'the thoughtless selfishness and indifference of men of all classes' was denounced in the nineties to Booth's collaborators. Housing had improved a great deal, but not to the extent of convincing the average English workman that any duty lay on him to remain in his house if he felt inclined to take his pleasure outside it, whether at football, betting, the pub, or the workmen's club where, like his social superiors, he could enjoy his drink and the society of his equals without the interference of the other sex.

Working men's clubs were something which the middle classes tried, and failed, to take over. Many were started with the idea of 'improving' the working classes, often in the direction of temperance, but the ones that succeeded were the independent ones, founded and run by working men themselves without any uplifting motive. They were not very well regarded by the more puritanically minded. A Congregationalist deacon who lived opposite one in London complained that 'the men used to turn out at from 12.30 to 2 in the morning and would join hands in the road and sing "Auld Lang Syne"'.

As the century died the demand for amusement increased. Music halls grew and flourished and 'the cinematograph and various forms of the phonograph' were seen in some of them. 'Excursions in brakes', it was said of London in the nineties, 'are without end.' One such excursion consisted of sixteen vehicles, 'containing all the girls from some large

Rev C. H. Spurgeon, preaching at the South London Baptist Tabernacle. The Tabernacle was said to hold 5,000 people, and Spurgeon could fill every seat in it. On 12th January 1869, Rev B. J. Armstrong, a country clergyman from Norfolk, went to discover, if possible, the secret of Spurgeon's power. 'He preaches from a huge balcony, up and down which he continually walks, addressing first one portion and then another of his vast congregation . . . His voice is powerful, but without sweetness or modulation of tone . . . There was nothing extraordinary in the address and the only clue that I could discover to the unbounded popularity of the man was his wonderful assurance. Walked all the way home, reflecting on so extraordinary a scene.'

works with their young men, as to whom all that the milkman, who was looking on, could say, was, "Well, they dress better, but their manners are about the same."' All this rose to its greatest height on Bank Holiday, and 'very rarely does one hear a good word for the Bank Holidays. The more common view is that they are a curse, and . . . the mischievous results from a sexual point of view . . . are frequently noted.' Respectability and middle-class morality, evidently, were apt to break down on Hampstead Heath on August Monday.

The strongest sanction for conventional morality was Christianity. In so far as there was organized, systematic Christianity among the working classes at all, it was to be found mainly among the Catholic Irish and, on the Protestant side, among the Primitive Methodists, whose affairs were organized by the working classes for themselves without that patronage from higher up the social scale which working men disliked and suspected. The Primitive Methodists were not numerous. In 1850 there were about 100,000 of them, and there were fewer, probably, later. Nor were they widespread, being strongest in the industrial north, particularly Sheffield and the Northumberland and Durham

coalfields. But they were closely associated with working-class efforts at self-improvement and with the leadership of trade unions. They were celebrated for their strictness, fervour and zeal, if not always for their learning. C. H. Spurgeon, the great mid-century Baptist preacher, who considered that he owed his conversion to an almost illiterate Primitive Methodist, had heard that their hymn-singing would make people's heads ache, and when that was combined with their love of preaching they were probably accurately, if not benevolently, described by their nickname of Prim Ranters.

The Prim Ranters and other devout working men were in a minority. A Roman priest told Charles Booth that 'England is perhaps christianized in her civilization, but it is not Christian.' A high Anglican parson took much the same view, saying, 'A few are caught young and kept, but for the most part both preaching and service are beyond them.' In general most observers throughout Victoria's reign agreed that true religion was a scarce commodity among the working classes and practically non-existent among the poor, especially in London. The only question was whether the masses had drifted away from the faith, possibly in the transition from country to town life, or whether they had ever been believers at all.

The attitude of the working classes and the poor towards the forces of organized religion was apt to be determined by their view of the social structure, not by questions of belief at all. They pretty generally identified the Churches— especially the Church of England—with the classes above them: something for the well-to-do, not for the ordinary man. Their view of middle and upper-class piety was not flattering. They knew of pious employers who sweated their workpeople; they saw churchgoers spending on luxuries (and on pew-rents) while they could themselves barely afford necessities. They saw no reason to spend Sunday, their day of rest and recreation, in church-going, which they thought of as neither. They preferred to get up late, have the best dinner of the week, and spend the rest of the day in drinking, in visiting or in family gatherings. Why should they go and listen to the parson who, they imagined, was well paid from the rates or from national funds of some kind and who need claim no particular virtue above other men, who also did what they were paid for?

This heathen world did not go unassailed. On the contrary, all the formidable apparatus of Victorian practical

piety was brought to bear on it through the parishes of the Establishment, through the priesthood of Rome, through the dissenting ministries, and through the missions and settlements of every denomination and of none. Missions could rouse temporary enthusiasm if they were exciting enough to burn up the drabness of everyday life. Individuals, especially the celibates of the High Church and of Rome, who were seen to be poor men living amongst the poor,

A curate in an industrial parish, from an engraving after John Leech, 1855. 'Town incumbents are always anxious to fill their churches for the sake of the pew-rents, and an eloquent curate is of course of service for that purpose . . .' (H. B. Thomson, 1857). It may be doubted whether this curate's eloquence is doing much to fill the parson's pews

could sometimes stir something deeper. But about most of this activity there was an aroma of patronage which the working classes resented. Although, often in unedifying rivalry, these various agencies of conversion pressed energetically towards the same goal they never, in Charles Booth's disenchanted view, came near achieving it. 'Among working men', as one of his informants put it, 'a kind of sublimated trade unionism is the most prevalent gospel: a vague bias towards that which is believed to be good for one's fellow men.'

'The summit of working-class life', in Booth's opinion, was reached with foremen and highly-paid artisans. These would be men earning between 40s. (£2.00) and 70s. (£3.50) a week, and other members of the household might bring in money too. 'They live very comfortably', said Booth, 'and many of them save money, or insure their lives for a considerable sum.' They were investors in the Post Office Savings Bank and in the friendly societies which, after a long history, had by the mid-eighties a membership running into millions. They might own their own houses, particularly in the provinces, and perhaps other people's houses, too. They were ambitious for themselves and their children. They were sober and steady, strict in their family life and impeccable in their morals. They might well be actively religious.

Between these people and 'the poor' there was a very great gulf, both in standards of living and in ways of thought, and there is no more hoary falsehood than the one about 'working-class solidarity'. Men of the same trade, provided they were in the same union, felt great mutual loyalty and would go to great lengths to uphold any cause which they had jointly undertaken, even against their own individual interests. This did not necessarily mean solidarity with men of other trades, who might be dangerous competitors, or with those below them in the social scale. The 'new unionism' of the eighties and later, fighting to organize the dockers, the match-girls and other neglected unfortunates, could count on very little support indeed from the members of the craft unions. The distinction between 'the working class' and 'the poor' was by no one felt so strongly as by the comfortable working class themselves. A product of the nineteenth century, and of the later nineteenth century at that, they had far greater affinities, unacknowledged though they might often be, with the masters of the nineteenth-century scene, the middle classes.

'In the front row at the opera'. Painting by William Holyoake.
'Royal Italian Opera or Covent Garden Theatre . . . With the
exception of the pantomime from Christmas to Easter, the only
theatrical representations are Italian operas, from August to November
the building is utilised for promenade concerts. Evening costume is
de rigueur, except in the gallery. Boxes from £2 2s [£2.10] to £12 12s
[£12.60], orchestra stalls 21s [£1.05], amphitheatre stalls 10s 6d [52½p]
and 5s [25p], pit 7s 6d [37½p], amphitheatre 2s 6d [12½p] . . . In winter,
stalls 7s [35p], dress circle 5s [25p], amphitheatre stalls 3s [15p], pit
2s 6d [12½p], gallery 1s [5p].' K. Baedeker, *London and its Environs,* 1879

7 The foundations of middle-class life

'And in this spirit he addressed them on more than one occasion ... pointing out that their happiness and well-being as individuals in after life, must necessarily depend mainly upon themselves—upon their own diligent self-culture, self-discipline, and self-control—and, above all, on that honest and upright performance of individual duty, which is the glory of manly character.' Thus Samuel Smiles, in 1859, expressed the central creed of the middle classes: that individual effort, backed by austerity of life, would propel any man, no matter what his origins, to success in this world and (Smiles might have added) if reinforced by the right brand of piety, to salvation in the next.

This, of course, was thoroughly subversive doctrine, since it struck at the roots of the traditional social system in which every man 'knew his place' and kept to it. But the sober, god-fearing family men who lived by it were saved from being conscious revolutionaries by an intense respect for the old system and an ambition to thrust themselves and their families into it, provided that it could be suitably modified to accommodate them. They were quite ruthless about that—the old social order *must* be modified—but, once modified, they wanted to inhabit it, not to overthrow it, and the story of the middle classes in Victorian England is very much the story of a take-over bid for the established order of society.

Their central principle was competition. They found a society in which most of the best things in life—wealth, property, social position—were conventionally regarded as belonging to those who were 'born to them'. They wanted to substitute for it a society in which those who had the ability might seize the prizes—and then enjoy them under a system of law which would still protect the rights of property. This new, competitive society was not at all to the liking of supporters of the old order. A Tory writer, about 1850, spoke of 'the system ... of leaving men to practise for their own advancement all arts save actual violence', and in this opinion he would no doubt have been echoed by men otherwise of a diametrically opposed turn of mind such as the early Socialists. But it was an unfashionable view, and it was not the view which, in the long run, was to prevail. The competitive society was on its way in, and Samuel Smiles's *Self-Help* ran to sales of 20,000 copies in its first year.

There was nothing new about the middle-class outlook. It would have been perfectly familiar to a seventeenth-century tradesman. But the new industrial order of things

Prosperity and domestic comfort, from a design by Lewis F. Day published in the *Magazine of Art*, 1881

put the middle classes in a position of unprecedented power and influence. They were able under Victoria to set the tone of the national life in a way that would have been inconceivable under George III.

The industrial world was run by the middle classes; as it grew, so did their opportunities. In the past the representative middle-class man—the shop-keeper, the merchant, the closely related banker—had been concerned with the sale of goods and the use of money, but not directly with manufacturing, which was the affair of craftsmen. There had been very little scope for middle-class technical or professional

employment. There were the skilled artisans on the one hand, the lawyers on the other; that was about all. But as factories went up, factory owners began to appear alongside merchants and bankers at the top of the middle-class tree. The whole scale and scope of commercial activity expanded; clerks, commercial travellers and technicians multiplied.

New professions came into being. The mechanical engineer, often a Northerner or a Scot, emerged from amongst blacksmiths and millwrights; the civil engineer from the designers of fortifications and other military works. Between them (often combined in one man) the two sorts of engineer equipped the factories and built the railways. By the fifties the accountant was distinct from the clerk; as firms grew and their finances became more complex his profession flourished.

Law and medicine, stimulated by commercial growth and by the growth in the number of people who could afford professional advice in their private affairs, grew in numbers, prosperity and reputation. The higher branches of the Civil Service, as government activity increased, came to offer an attractive career to the middle-class intellectual, especially after most branches of the Service had been thrown open to competition in the seventies.

But to take advantage of all this, the middle class had to reshape society in their own interests. Previously they had got on as best they could in a world ruled by aristocratic and rural interests. George Eliot, in *Middlemarch*, looked back from the seventies at middle-class life in the thirties. What she saw was the tradesmen and bankers of a country town in business to serve the surrounding gentry, and completely subordinate to them. Of a middle class independent of the landowners she gives no hint, although her story partly turns on the agitation for the Reform Act of 1832, that great political victory of the middle classes. But there was much, much more to do before England could become a place fit for an ambitious lad to practise self-help in.

How, to start with, could he get the kind of schooling he needed to fit him for trade, industry or the professions? The greatest prestige in the educational world attached to the ancient public schools, with their rigidly classical curriculum and their anti-commercial outlook, scornful alike of money-making, technology and science. They were emphatically not designed to cater for the rising middle classes and never in Victoria's reign did they admit that commerce or industry could really be a fit occupation for a gentleman.

149

Which was a pity, for the Victorian self-made man, greatly desirous of having his sons accepted as gentlemen, was apt to have them educated at these establishments if he could afford to, and so they were disabled from taking up the kind of work on which the country increasingly depended for its livelihood.

The public schools were a specialized kind of grammar school, and it was the grammar schools, before the industrial age, which had provided for that very small minority who were considered to need educating above the most elementary stage. All social classes—even, in some schools, both sexes—had sat together, and together they had ground through the universal classical curriculum. The tradesman's son had usually left before the son of a gentleman who was going on to the university, but the grounding of both

Stephenson's locomotive manufactory, Newcastle on Tyne, from *The Illustrated London News*, 1864. The factory opened in 1824, being financed by George Stephenson (£1,000), Edward Pease, his backer (£500), and Thomas Richardson (£500). In 1827 Pease wrote to Robert Stephenson, then in Colombia, 'I can assure thee that thy business at Newcastle, as well as thy father's engineering, have suffered very much from thy absence, and, unless thou soon return, the former will be given up . . .' Samuel Smiles, *George and Robert Stephenson*, 1879

had been the same, and if the lower-class boy had shown a marked academic bent it had not been too difficult for him to follow the young squire to Oxford or Cambridge. The school education and often exhibitions or sizarships to the university had been paid for out of the founder's endowments or out of other benefactions, so that as long as a boy's parents could keep him and forgo his earnings they had to find no other money, or only trifling sums. The whole system had been closely tied into local life, with places at school and exhibitions to the university restricted to boys from the neighbourhood of the school.

By the time Victoria came to the throne the grammar schools were much decayed. Their endowments, stated in sums related to the money values of the sixteenth and seventeenth centuries, had become absurdly small. Under Elizabeth I, apparently, you could get a good schoolmaster for £10 a year. Under Victoria the head of a first-class school could get £1,000; of a second-class school, perhaps half that or rather more. Neither figure was remotely possible from most endowments. Nor would endowments, generally speaking, allow proper upkeep of buildings or the engagement of assistant masters. The deficiencies were widely met by allowing the head and other masters to take boarders—a most profitable proposition—and to charge fees, but then the establishment would be on its way to becoming a 'public' school open to boys from the country at large, which was precisely what the grammar school, a designedly local institution, was not.

Moreover, the law only allowed the grammar schools to apply their endowments to the teaching of the classics. Anything else had to be paid for out of fees. The classics, useless intellectual lumber as they were for most boys, made small appeal to the practical middle-class mind, but the middle classes put up with them as long as the process of learning them brought their sons in contact with the gentry and hence with the source of patronage and profitable employment. When the sons of gentlemen forsook the grammar schools for the public schools the middle-class attitude changed. 'Many in the middle classes', as the Taunton Commissioners of 1868 reported, 'are not content with Latin and Greek when Latin and Greek no longer means association with the sons of the gentry.' What the middle classes wanted were useful commercial subjects—above all, arithmetic—or, at a higher level, subjects that would be useful in competitive and qualifying examina-

(Overleaf)
Lesson in the open air: a photograph by Octavius Hill, c 1845

Private education, from an engraving after Charles Keene, 1882

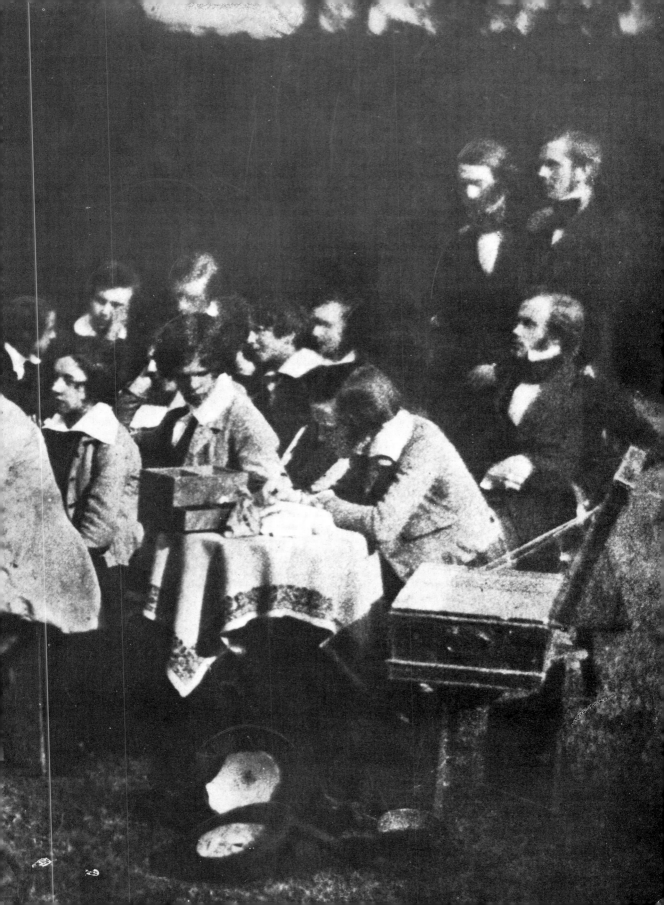

tions: something that had not been dreamt of by the grammar schools' pious founders. Moreover, a good many worthy middle-class dissenters objected to schools that were so closely tied, as grammar schools usually were, to the Established Church.

By the middle of Victoria's reign, many grammar schools had dwindled to grubby squalor in unfashionable districts. Their buildings, almost certainly old, would probably be tumbledown and their masters, quite possibly, likewise. The general condition of Lancashire grammar school buildings in the sixties was 'ugly without and dirty within'; as to masters, those in more than a quarter of the grammar schools in Suffolk were described as follows: 'At one, the

The New Reading Grammar School, 'constructed by trustees under an Act of Parliament obtained in 1867 for the purpose of establishing at Reading a thoroughly efficient and useful school . . . with a more enlarged scope than the ancient grammar school of that town. The object sought was the providing the means of a thorough middle-class education, to be supplemented by a lower school for the education and benefit of the poorer classes, and through which their children might have the opportunity of

154

rising gradually to the principal school, and the more deserving and gifted of them to be thus enabled to secure all the advantages of the higher establishment.' (*The Illustrated London News*, 16th September 1871)

master . . . supports old age in the comfortable schoolhouse: at another, he was almost helpless from old age and paralysis; at a third, he was honest enough to declare that he was no longer fit for work; at a fourth, he was deaf; while at three others he was . . . languishing under his work.' Since masters held office for life, they could not be sacked, and since there was no provision for a pension, they could not often be induced to resign.

Many grammar schools had declined towards the elementary level, such as the one at Tadcaster where, in the sixties, 'only one child in the upper division . . . could write from dictation a sentence of words of one syllable without mistakes'. Others had lost their pupils. There were only six at Ottery St Mary about 1868, all very young, and where the boarders should have had their dining room the master kept two carriages. At Whitgift's Hospital, Croydon, a master found no pupils when he came and left none when he died, thirty years later. As things were in the first thirty years of Queen Victoria's reign, the only parents who cared to take up the free places at a grammar school were either the poorest or those who cared least for their children's education.

Even if all the grammar schools had been good, there would not have been enough, nor would they have been in the right places, for the towns and parts of towns where they had been needed in the sixteenth, seventeenth and eighteenth centuries were not those where they were needed in the nineteenth. Private schools had sprung up to fill the gaps.

These were profit-making institutions which had to supply what the customers thought they wanted. That, generally speaking, was vocational training and a desirable social background. That meant a background no lower than the parents' own and as much above it as they could afford. With other aspects of education, in the view of contemporary observers, middle-class parents were not greatly concerned. They wanted their boys taught enough English to write business letters and very good arithmetic, which many of them looked upon as the most important subject of all. Hence the kind of school which H. G. Wells went to in the later seventies—Morley's Commercial Academy at Bromley, Kent—where the owner taught twenty-five to thirty-five boys single-handed in a single room, laying great stress on 'copperplate flourishes, long addition sums and bookkeeping'.

Wells had a certain respect for old Morley, and it is important not to dismiss Victorian private schools as wholly inefficient and corrupt, though doubtless many were both. They were often kept by graduates of London or the Scottish universities—men who knew what education ought to be, even if parents often crippled their efforts to supply it, and in the better schools new methods, new subjects and educational experiments generally were tried which would have been impossible elsewhere. Moreover, the dearer private schools had excellent buildings, equipment and food, because in these matters parents could form a very shrewd idea as to whether they were getting their money's worth. 'There are establishments in Yorkshire', said the Commissioners of 1868, '. . . on a large and costly scale, with the newest educational appliances, the most perfect drill grounds and gymnasia, large cricket fields and baths; and arrangements for health, comfort, and instruction which evince great administrative power, and require large capital and incessant supervision to keep them efficient.'

But the cheaper the worse, especially schools serving parents too ill-educated to recognize a bad school when they saw it. The assistant masters, in particular, were a seedy bunch. Their pay was low, so was their social position, and their prospects amounted to nothing at all—they were simply part of their principals' 'money-making machinery'. 'In my examinations', reported one official enquirer, 'I not unfrequently found them fragrant of alcohol.'

Girls were even worse served than boys. They were generally supposed to be less in need of 'mental cultivation' than boys, and less capable of it, and too much education was thought to ruin their prospects in the marriage market. On the other hand they were expected to have certain 'accomplishments', particularly music and drawing, and a smattering of ill-assorted, undigested general knowledge, ranging from the dates of the Kings of England to the origins of guano. 'The ideal presented to a young girl', as one female writer of the sixties bitterly remarked, 'is to be amiable, inoffensive, always ready to give pleasure and to be pleased.' There was no real tradition of girls' schooling, as there was of boys', because girls of the higher classes had always been educated at home—as, during the greater part of Victoria's reign, most of them continued to be.

Faced with thoroughly unsatisfactory opportunities for educating their sons and daughters, the early Victorians responded by founding proprietary schools—a remedy en-

156

The Rugby match, by J. M. Cronheim. 'The [Rugby] Union code [of 1871] very properly abolished hacking, tripping and scragging, the last of which practices consisted in the twisting of an opponent's neck round, with a grip of the arm, to make him cry "down" if he had any available voice; but the abolition of these practices, and especially of the "hacking," tended to make the game "tight" and to render of little value the best and most skilful forward play, which can be only exhibited in "loose" scrummages.' *Football*, in the Badminton Library, 1904

tirely in keeping with the principles of *Self-Help*. These schools were privately owned, but not by a single individual who had his living to make. Their purpose was education, not profit, though many were first financed by shareholders who drew a small return on their capital. They thus avoided the over-riding necessity of making money—one of the worst drawbacks of the private schools—and they had some independence of the whims and prejudices of parents. Nevertheless, taking one thing with another they had to please their customers, so that they avoided the torpor of the grammar schools. They commonly provided more or less handsomely for 'modern subjects' which did not fit into the classical traditions of the public schools, because the great spur to their foundation was the growing system of public examinations, especially, in the first place, those for entry into the Royal Military Academy at Woolwich, for the training of gunner and engineer officers, and for the Indian Civil Service.

Many proprietary schools were founded from the thirties onward, especially after 1840 as the spreading railways began to make boarding schools increasingly accessible. Between them they covered the whole social, religious and educational range of the middle classes. Marlborough (1843) and a few others were avowedly reproductions of the ancient public schools, organized so that the fees could be lower, and in them the classics were administered undiluted to the sons of comparatively impoverished gentry, especially parsons' sons. Others, like University College School (1830), Cheltenham (1841) and Brighton (1845) adulterated the classics with pretty strong doses of modern subjects, and Cheltenham, in particular, built a reliable road to Woolwich. There were other recognized 'Army' schools, but from the more devotedly classical schools it long remained necessary for a boy to go to a 'crammer' if he seriously intended to go into the Army, and professional education was almost entirely a matter of apprenticeship or 'articles'—a revealing comment on the awkward relationship between 'liberal education' and the demands of the workaday world.

The highest purpose of education, at any rate in theory, was religious, and there were schools to suit every variety of English Christianity. The Dissenters carried on an old tradition in new foundations like Mill Hill (1807) and Taunton (1847). At the Catholic end of the scale, schools like Douai came out of exile and set up, at last, on English soil. Most schools had an Anglican bias but at least one—

158

John Hughes.

MORDEN HALL
Boarding School, Surrey,
FOR
YOUNG GENTLEMEN,
Conducted by
Mr Thomas N. White

Morden Hall Boarding School for
Young Gentlemen, from its
prospectus of 1850

University College School—made a point of having no
religious associations at all. It is curious that the Jews, with
their respect for education and their intense family life and
religious feeling, made no effort to provide proprietary
schools for themselves, or at any rate nothing on the scale
of the Christian denominations.

Occupational groups were catered for as well as religious
beliefs. Parsons' sons were provided for at Marlborough,
doctors' sons at Epsom (1853), commercial travellers' sons
at Pinner, and the sons of clerks, small shopkeepers and
even 'upper artisans' at establishments much lower down
the line. Some of these, which were all day schools, had
developed from mechanics' institutes taken over (as
mechanics' institutes tended to be) by the lower middle class.
Others were sectarian foundations, Anglican or nonconformist.

The toilet: colour plate from Mrs Beeton's *Housewife's Treasury*. 'If a lady's-maid can afford it, we would advise her to initiate herself in the mysteries of hairdressing before entering on her duties. If a mistress finds her maid handy, and willing to learn, she will not mind the expense of a few lessons, which are almost necessary, as the fashion and mode of dressing the hair is continually changing.' *Mrs Beeton's Book of Household Management*. 1895 edn.

Girls, at last, were seriously provided for in proprietary schools. Queen's College, Harley Street, was founded in 1848; the North London Collegiate School in 1850; Cheltenham Ladies' College in 1853. At all these, and at others, the 'slovenliness and showy superficiality' of 'Middle-Class Female Education' (to quote the report of the Schools Enquiry Commission, 1868) were fiercely repressed. The result could be a régime so ruled and regulated that all the life was squeezed out of it, and particular scorn was poured on the idea of girls making themselves pleasing to men. But

Visiting a girls' school: an engraving of 1850

it did become possible for a few girls—at the start a very few
—to get the same kind of intellectual training as their
brothers, which was widely regarded as unladylike and
probably bad for their health.

By 1868 there were about 4,600 boarders at proprietary
schools and about 7,600 day boys. In the view of the Commissioners who in that year reported on them, they represented an effort to replace the failing grammar schools, and
'the reforms which they were intended to introduce have to
a great degree become recognized as in the main right'.
Certainly this was the general feeling of the day, and as the
grammar schools were taken in hand and reorganized, one
by one, during the latter part of the century, many of them
became indistinguishable in teaching, administration and
general atmosphere from the more recently founded 'proprietary' schools. Each took something over from the other
and both drew heavily on the reformed tradition of the
public schools.

The Commissioners' criticism of the proprietary schools,
and it might equally be applied to many of the rejuvenated
grammar schools which followed the same pattern, was that

they were 'class schools'. They represented middle-class determination to get education suited to middle-class pursuits, but they also represented middle-class social ambitions so that at the more pretentious, such as Cheltenham or Clifton, no tradesman's son would be admitted—certainly not the son of a tradesman in the town. This, in the Commissioners' view, made proprietary schools unfit to rank as 'public' schools, which was ironic, since in the last thirty years or so of Victoria's reign they increasingly took to themselves the use of that name.

With good solid schooling behind him the Victorian middle-class lad could confidently start looking for his livelihood. The prosperous tradesman's son might stay at school until he was sixteen or thereabouts and then set to learning the family business, which had been the middle-class way for generations. Without family interest or without capital his prospects in business would be poor, unless he was exceptionally enterprising, able or lucky, for salaried employment above the miserable level of the clerk or shop assistant was rare. Most firms were run by their owners who took care to keep the best jobs for themselves and their relations (including relations by marriage). Although the Victorian middle classes were against patronage when it lay in hands other than their own, especially aristocratic hands, it did not at all follow that they would apply the same principle to patronage which they themselves controlled. It was almost hopeless for an outsider to try to break into the higher management of, say, brewing, the London coal trade, banking, or virtually any other established and prosperous activity. When, from time to time, a new man did fight himself into a position of strength, the ring would open just wide enough to admit him (and his family) and then close again.

There was, however, an alternative, which the Victorian middle classes did a great deal to develop, and this was to seek a professional qualification which would make its holder as independent as he could reasonably hope to be of the need for influence or family connections, though both were extremely useful if you had them. It is not quite true to say that the Victorians invented the professions, but it is true that they extended them, provided them with a good deal of *mystique*, tradition and snobbery and left them altogether stronger and more venerated than they found them. The professions, along with the public schools, became part of the essential fabric of middle-class life, and to become a professional man represented the height of ambition for boys born a little too far down the middle-class scale for comfort.

The solidest reason for seeking a professional qualification, especially if it carried a legally entrenched right to practise, was that it gave the surest possible hope of a secure livelihood. Like the skilled artisan who had served his apprenticeship, the doctor, lawyer, clergyman or engineer 'had a living in his hands' which nothing but villainous ill-luck, gross incompetence or crime was likely to take away. Moreover, once the framework of qualifying exams, had been set up, a professional qualification depended on ability alone (even if only the ability to pass exams), and not on 'influence', patronage or wealth. It was an essential weapon in the middle-class struggle to throw profitable careers open to talent. And the knowledge that one had the ability to 'qualify' was a useful boost to a young man's self-confidence at the beginning, just as, later, the consciousness of being a skilled practitioner of some difficult art added to the established man's self-respect.

Almost equally important, professional status was a marriage between gentility and trade which the middle-class mind found highly congenial. The middle classes were built on trade and were loth to sacrifice its profits, but trade had a dubious social standing. The younger sons of the gentry had not, in the past, found it beneath their dignity to join some flourishing merchant firm, and the gentry—the nobility even—had never scorned rich merchants' daughters for their brides. But riches lent enchantment to the view; the great merchant had enough money to live like a gentleman and conceal his origins. Not so with your shopkeeper or petty trader who, besides, cultivated an undignified and ingratiating manner towards his customers. Not so with your rough northern manufacturer, newly sprung from the lower middle class or worse. 'Trade' in general, unless profitable enough to provide an income comparable with that from a landed estate, was no occupation for a gentleman, and, in view of some trade practices, understandably so.

The professional man, though still inspired by the profit motive, undertook to observe rules of conduct which a tradesman might ignore, though exactly what the rules were it was not always easy to define. They certainly did not stand in the way of making money. A writer of 1850 quoted the income of a rising barrister at £5,000: of 'a physician

who is becoming popular' at £1,000 more. The professional man, at some sacrifice of his freedom of action, might rank as a gentleman without being a penny the worse off than if he had been 'in trade'—indeed, he might do a great deal better—and that was exactly what the ambitious middle-class man wanted, if not for himself, then for his sons. Hence the energy put into the cultivation of old professions and the launching of new ones, and into setting up an educational system which would serve professional needs.

But what was a profession? Divinity, physic and law would have been an earlier generation's answer, but the matter was not so simple as that. Take 'law', for example. Nobody doubted the dignity of bench and bar, but attorneys were a different matter. 'They are of various grades', wrote a barrister of 1850, 'from the low, rapacious pettifogger, who grasps at three-and-sixpenny fees, and is something between the common cur and bulldog of the law, up to the finished gentleman, who has in his hands the most important affairs, and is professionally acquainted with the most delicate secret histories of the first families of the land.' Amongst newer occupations the engineers early made out a claim to

In the divorce court, about 1880. Until 1857 divorce was only possible by private Act of Parliament after proceedings in the Church courts, and it was not granted on equal terms to men and women until 1923. Reports of divorce proceedings provided excellent pornography until the Regulation of Reports Act 1926 prohibited the publication of indecent details and restricted the report of matrimonial causes to certain specified particulars

Medical students at St Thomas's, from an engraving in *The Graphic*, October, 1886. 'It is only after years of patient study, pursued at the cost of great mental and physical labour, that the student is entitled to present himself for examination.' *The Lancet*, 1860

professional standing, but again there was a cleavage, for the civil engineers considered themselves superior to the mechanical. Then there was teaching; what was one to say of that? No one doubted the social position of masters at the public schools. They were mostly, in any case, Anglican clergy. But teaching shaded away down, by imperceptible degrees, to wretched drunken ushers in back-street private schools; could they claim professional status? Most teachers, anyway, were women, which raised a very awkward problem: was the professional woman a possible animal?

Matters of status were seriously regarded. Escott, in his survey of England, devoted several pages to discussing it and concluded, amongst other things, that professions like the bar, where fees did not pass directly from client to practitioner, ranked higher than professions like medicine, where they did. It was also, in his view, a slight mark of inferiority if a professional man had the right to recover his fees by legal process. The whole thing ought rather to proceed on the fiction that the transaction—in law, medicine or whatever it might be—was simply an exercise of friendship by one gentleman on behalf of another, to be rewarded or not as the beneficiary might decide. This may have been a rarified view, but the marks of professional status, whatever they might be, were sought after by the practitioners of one occupation after another, until by the end of the century the ancient three had been multiplied many times.

The professionalizers' greatest triumph was their transformation of the medical profession. In 1800 only the two Royal Colleges (of Physicians and Surgeons) and the Society of Apothecaries made any pretence to provide systematic medical education, and nothing like modern examinations existed. The fellowship of the College of Physicians conferred social standing, but it was not for the ordinary general practitioner. He might have qualified with the Surgeons or the Apothecaries, but his knowledge would have been picked up as an apprentice or in practice, with little or no formal instruction. He was subject to no controlling body and was unrecognized in law. The surgeon's trade, before anaesthetics, was rough. Anybody could set up in it, and 'sawbones' was unlikely to be a gentleman.

Against the hostility of the Physicians and with little help from the Surgeons, a movement began which in 1815 produced the Apothecaries Act: the first Act to give statutory backing to proper professional education, tested by qualifying examinations which conferred legally protected rights of practice. Medical students of the better sort went abroad and to Scotland: in England medical schools were set up in defiance of the Colleges. By 1858 twenty-one authorities could grant licences to practice—some general, some specialized, some geographically restricted, some valid throughout the United Kingdom.

In 1858, after twenty years of effort, a Medical Act was passed. It did away with training by apprenticeship and called for 'an elaborate series of lectures' instead. It set up the Medical Register and placed severe restrictions on unregistered practitioners. To enforce this newly established discipline it set up the General Medical Council, a body found from within the profession itself, which wielded as its principal weapon the right to 'strike off'.

The Census Report of 1871 recorded that in the ten years from 1861 'medical men remained nearly stationary [in numbers]: the qualification having been much raised', and that was undoubtedly a direct result of the Act. With the raising of qualifications the general standing of doctors in the community rose as well, and it came to be no longer a

matter of wonder that a man of good family like Doctor Thorne in Trollope's novel should become a country practitioner. But the process was a slow one, for quacks did not disappear all at once, and even as late as Escott's time, twenty years or more after the passing of the Act, the general practitioner—'the lineal successor of the apothecary'—does

A dentist at work, from an engraving after George du Maurier, 1882. Dentists were hardly respectable, professionally, until the Dentists' Act, 1878, provided for registration after examination

not seem quite to have made good his position.

The 1858 Medical Act gave precise expression to the professional idea. It established three great principles—qualification by examination, a legally entrenched right to practise, and the right of a profession to internal self-government. It raised the whole standing of the medical profession by insisting on proper qualifications and at the same time it conferred on those who obtained them protection against unqualified competition. After it was passed, 'professional status' had a legal form and others who desired it had a model to copy. They were many, for its advantages were great.

Proprietary schools were being founded in great numbers in the forties and fifties. The competitive examination for entry into the Indian Civil Service was established by law in 1853. In 1854 Sir Charles Trevelyan and Sir Stafford Northcote recommended a similar competition for entry into the Civil Service at home. The first Medical Act was passed in 1858. In the sixties the country's schools were very thoroughly investigated by Royal Commissions and important reforms followed. Between 1855 and 1870 the Northcote-Trevelyan recommendations for competitive entry into the Civil Service came gradually into effect, and in 1871 the purchase of commissions in the Army was abolished, to be replaced by a system based on examinations.

In all these things the vigorous middle-class mind can be seen at work, moulding the life of Victorian England. Competition in a clear field is the great principle; patronage, privilege and 'influence' are to be detested and got rid of. Ancient institutions must be examined, reshaped, brought up to date; new ones must be invented if nothing old will do. At the roots of it all lay the determination to give education a strong shove in the direction of the 'useful arts' and to organize middle-class occupations on a basis of strength, efficiency and social recognition. By 1870 or thereabouts the foundations had been laid. The second generation of the Victorian middle class was about to enter on a world designed very much according to middle-class ideas.

8 Middle-class England

'Creatures of the inferior races eat and drink; only man dines. . . . Dining is the privilege of civilisation. The rank which people occupy in the grand scale may be measured by their way of taking their meals, as well as by their way of treating their women. The nation which knows how to dine has learnt the leading lesson of progress. It implies both the will and the skill to reduce to order, and surround with idealisms and graces the more material conditions of human existence; and wherever that will and that skill exist, life cannot be wholly ignoble.'
Mrs Beeton's Book of Household Management, 1895 edition

By setting up schools and by organizing the professions the middle classes gave themselves the means to get 'a start in life'. From this base, again in their own idiom, they 'got on'. Socially, that meant moving from manual occupations into 'trade'; from 'trade' into 'the professions'; from 'the professions', ultimately, into 'Society', where a gentleman's income was assumed to come from his estate. The middle classes might dislike the upper-class way of doing things as long as they felt themselves hindered by it, but that did not for one moment dim their ambition to join the upper class themselves if they could.

Middle-class life, therefore, was very largely an attempt to reach out towards gentility and to imprint the notions of the rural gentry upon the instincts of town-bred business men. But to say that the middle classes set out to imitate their betters is to over-simplify. There were many aspects of upper-class life which they could not approve of, and they were far too strong-minded to give up firmly held convictions. As they penetrated the upper levels of society they carried a good deal of luggage, and if upper-class ideas began to modify their own, so also their habits of thought impinged on those above them. More peers conducted family prayers in the nineteenth century, probably, than in the eighteenth.

Religion, especially nonconformity—'Chapel' as opposed to 'Church'—lay at the heart of middle-class life, as it had since the seventeenth century. Indeed the generally puritan and serious tone which the Victorians took pride in having reintroduced into English life was perhaps the greatest part of the middle-class triumph. It owed little to the upper classes, who for the most part were converted to that kind of Christianity unwillingly and late. It owed nothing to the poor who, below the level of working-class comfort, were mostly never converted to any kind of Christianity at all.

Most middle-class nonconformists were in three great camps—Congregationalists, Baptists and Wesleyan (not Primitive) Methodists—with a formidable outpost in the Evangelical wing of the Church of England. Beneath differences of organization and doctrine which do not concern us here the members of these groups had a similarity of outlook recognized in the phrase 'the nonconformist conscience', but each group had its own strongly marked individual character.

The direct descendants of early English puritanism were the Congregationalists or Independents. 'Ours', one of their

172

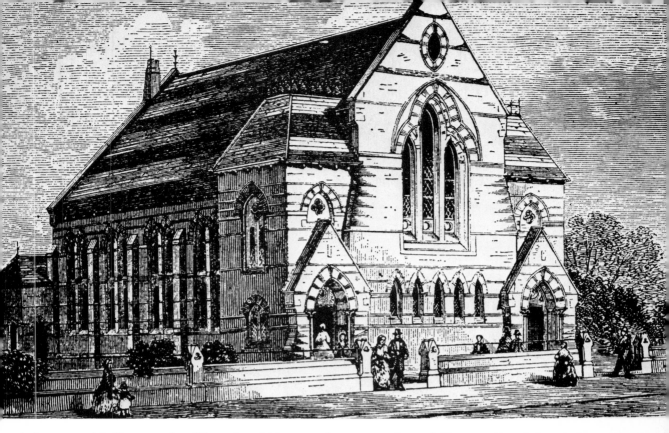

A Congregational chapel at Reading, designed in 1871, to hold 640 people. Engraving from *The Baptist Handbook* of 1871

ministers said, 'is not the Church of the poor', a remark which Charles Booth, for whose benefit it was made, considered an understatement. The Congregationalists were particularly strong among the middle classes of the great towns, and self-help and self-reliance were of the essence of their teaching. Each congregation was independent of all others: each chose its own pastor, ran its own affairs, decided its own doctrine and recognized no superior religious authority on earth.

The pastor of a prosperous congregation would be well paid—better, probably, than many a clergyman of the Establishment—and a great deal of the day-to-day business of running the affairs of the congregation would be taken on by elected deacons. The pastor would be left to take the lead among his people, to inspire their lives, to preach. From the pulpit in his low-domed, galleried church he would conduct an intensely personal service, running through prayers, lessons, hymns and notices to the climax of the sermon. Into all these things, but especially the prayers and the sermon, the pastor could pour himself; he had no set liturgy either to restrict or to support his personality.

In the street, after the service, the people would not hurry

away, for the Congregationalists had a busy social life, especially among the young, and much of what they did had only a rather tenuous connection with religion. There might be a Literary Society, a Literary Society's Lawn Tennis Club, a Camera Club, apart from more obviously religious activities such as a Young People's Society of Christian Endeavour, and meetings of one sort or another would run right through the year. 'The sociability of the [tennis] club', says one report of Congregationalist social activities, quoted by Booth, 'depends a great deal upon teas', and of the Camera Club the same report says 'Mr H. B. L. . . . offered as a special prize one of his celebrated pictures, a framed carbon enlargement of the late Lord Leighton's "Arab Hall" . . . which did not, however, receive the response it deserved.'

This is not a picture of an unbearably austere way of life, and indeed Booth makes it clear that he considered the Congregationalists' religious life of his time—the eighties— tranquil to the point of smugness, with few religious doubts and little intensity of experience. The influence of the Congregationalists, he concluded, 'is more social than religious, but it is good and wholesome, and being without exaltation is free from the dangers of reaction'. The Congregationalists were still capable of expressing themselves strongly on public questions, and another observer of the late seventies and eighties, Escott, thought them more active politically than either of the other two main nonconformist bodies, the Baptists and the Wesleyans.

The Baptist frame of mind was far more austere than the Congregationalist. 'Hell', says Booth, 'plays fully as great a part as Heaven; pleasure is distrusted as a wile of the Devil, and the personality of the Evil One retains a reality which in the case of the other sects has begun to fade.' Preaching in the nineties, a Baptist pastor said: 'Oh, man and woman, I pray you, in the name of my God, tonight, that you will face this matter and picture your own death-bed if you are not right with God . . . that relentless power that you have defied takes you shrinking to the edge of that abyss, and you shriek "I will not die!" You fall into that darkness of an unprepared Eternity! Oh, man, get ready! Time is flying, men are dying, hell is filling, Christ is coming, and you are unsaved— unready.'

Of the three great nonconformist churches the Wesleyan Methodists, in Booth's opinion, took a more joyous view of life than either of the other two. They could find a legitimate place for pleasure and their services made great use of music. The Baptists only hesitantly admitted any instrument beyond a tuning-fork to their worship and suspected choirs and part-singing as practices associated with priestcraft and prelacy, but the Wesleyans would have a full choir of both sexes, an organ, perhaps an orchestra as well. 'God is a God of gladness', said a Wesleyan monthly magazine, 'joyousness, light, love, beauty; every bright colour in the universe has been placed there by the hand of God, every strain of

Middle-class social life: a tennis party, from an engraving by George du Maurier, 1882

175

music, every ray of light, every brilliant gem reveals the hand of the Great Artist.' This somewhat fevered joyousness was probably an expression of 'high' Methodism, if such a phrase is permissible. At the 'lower' end of the doctrinal scale, which tended to be the lower end of the social scale also, there were many Methodists who kept to a simple form of service and a correspondingly severe outlook. But many of the better-off Methodist 'classes' did not differ greatly in doctrine, in liturgy, and in their taste in church architecture from the Church of England.

Many among the Evangelicals of the established Church, in fact, found themselves in greater sympathy with non-conformists, especially Wesleyans, than with their own High Church party. It was hardly surprising, since Wesleyan-ism and Evangelicalism were really two wings of one move-ment which, with strong middle-class support, had started transforming the religious life of the country well back in the eighteenth century. The middle classes, in fact, dealt with the Church as they dealt with other national institu-tions. They did their best, with considerable success, to impose their own views upon it and transform it from the inside. This made it all the easier for the rising middle-class family to transfer itself from the chapel to the parish church as it climbed the social ladder. And this was just what many middle-class families did, for the church was identified with all that was socially desirable in a way that the chapel was not.

Religiously speaking, then, the middle classes lay across the line that separated the Church from Dissent. Most of their weight and all their tradition lay on the dissenting side, which gave them a set of principles high, rigid and narrow. By these they guided, or failed to guide, their own lives and expected the rest of the nation to guide theirs. They brought them to public notice especially on Sunday, when many normally unexceptionable or even praiseworthy activities became sinful and religious observances were obligatory. In a respectable household there would be church or chapel twice in the day. No work would be done. There would be precious little play, for only the solemnest litera-ture would be permitted and only the most decorous games, amongst which some families would include Noah's Ark for the sake of its indubitable religious associations.

The Sunday frame of mind, for many people, was merely an accentuation of the suspicion which they normally felt to-wards any kind of activity which was neither 'work' nor

Sunday church-going, from an engraving after J. E. Millais, 1862. A census of church attendance was taken on Sunday, 30th March 1851, from which it was estimated that 7,333,564 people went to church that day while '5,288,294 persons, able to attend religious worship at least once, neglected altogether to do so.' The total population of England and Wales was 17,927,609

'religion': in other words, towards any kind of pleasure indulged in for its own sake. Thus in many middle-class households, particularly in the earlier part of Victoria's reign, cards, dancing and the theatre, besides being unthinkable on Sunday, were forbidden during the rest of the week also: a direct legacy from seventeenth-century puritanism. And to these ancient prohibitions the Victorians added a new one of their own—'temperance'.

The Victorian middle classes were quite properly shocked by drunkenness, and especially by its increase amongst the working classes (the upper classes had never made much pretence at sobriety) as they became more prosperous. But the remedy which many of them proposed, and which they

A temperance meeting: engraving after Richard Doyle, 1840

managed to go quite a long way towards enforcing by legislation, showed fanaticism of an intensity rare in English public life. With their propensity for judging everything in moral terms, they denounced drunkards as weaklings unable to put up a proper fight against temptation, without stopping to reflect that influences outside a man's control might drive him to drink. Although their ancestors, generally speaking, had accepted alcoholic drink without question, they began to denounce it as an unmitigated evil and tried to get as many people as possible to renounce it utterly.

Never was a movement so misnamed as the full-blown 'temperance' movement, for its aim—total abstinence—was intemperate in the extreme. It was something quite new in English life, for although social reformers had long condemned gin and other spirits, they had generally recognized beer as a cheap and wholesome drink, greatly to be preferred to impure water supplies, and the brewers, on the whole, had been regarded as social benefactors rather than the reverse. But from the fifties onwards, with increasing force, temperance propagandists ranged the brewers alongside the distillers and attacked them accordingly. They found support particularly in Lancashire and Yorkshire, in Wales, in Cornwall and in East Anglia—all areas where nonconformity was strong—and, socially, especially among the lower middle class and the 'respectable artisans' enfranchised in 1867. But the movement was far more than a local one, far more than a quirk of one social group. Its support was widespread and its successes were notable. Much of what was achieved, such as restrictions on the sale of drink to children, was highly desirable. Much of what was proposed was unreasonable and often represented an attempt to interfere with other people's liberty 'for their own good'. All in all, the temperance movement was a formidable demonstration of the power of organized middle-class opinion and of 'the nonconformist conscience'.

As 'temperance' represented one aspect of the self-control so much admired and sought after by the middle classes, so their sexual morality represented another. Here again, as in so many other things, the middle classes found themselves uneasily poised between those above them and those below, whose practice, if not their doctrine, was directly opposed to the middle classes' own. The upper classes, accustomed to pleasing themselves, did not entirely give up pleasing themselves even when the influence of puritan morality was at its height, though they found it prudent to be more than ordinarily wary of being found out. Amongst the poor, notions of marriage were apt to be hazy, illegitimate children were tolerantly accepted, and pregnancy very commonly came before the wedding. 'Girls of this class', says Booth, 'do not lose caste because of an illegitimate child. A young mother bringing an illegitimate child to be registered will be accompanied by two or three companions.'

No such easy-going attitudes as these were possible for the devout and serious middle classes, nor indeed for the 'respectable' working classes. Sexual experience, especially for women, should be contained wholly within marriage, and sexual pleasure, even married sexual pleasure (again, especially for women), was widely held to be sinful, so that it was best, on the whole, to be as ignorant of these matters as possible and not to talk of them at all, at any rate in mixed company or in front of the children.

Behind this iron orthodoxy there was, no doubt, a good deal of less inhibited behaviour. Taine, visiting England in the sixties, thought that married women were nearly all faithful. Nevertheless, well-to-do shopkeepers' wives, having plenty of servants to do their house work and little else to occupy them, sometimes found 'the great emptiness of boredom . . . a wide open door to seduction'. And prostitution seems to have been a fairly flourishing trade, with clients among the most respectable. The Royal Commissioners who reported on Oxford University in 1852 considered 'sensual vice' one of the most obvious of the 'existing evils' there, and said that opportunities for it were 'too abundant' in the villages round Oxford and elsewhere outside the Proctors' jurisdiction—a revealing comment on a university whose students were mostly intending to take Holy Orders. In London, Taine noticed that shops and more or less respectable houses in the Strand and Haymarket advertised 'beds to let' by day; in the evening 'the mature man, the young man of the respectable classes' might be seen entering and leaving in considerable numbers. In 1882 a select committee of the House of Lords remarked that 'juvenile prostitution, from an almost incredibly early age, is increasing to an appalling extent . . . especially in London'.

What struck Taine most forcibly, however, was not so much irregular behaviour, either with prostitutes or in genuine love affairs, as the extreme guiltiness which an Englishman felt at indulging in it. 'An Englishman in a state of adultery', he noted, 'is miserable: even at the supreme

moment his conscience torments him.' Quite how he came by this last piece of information is mysterious, but in the general tone of his remark he may well have been right. He had observed that English life, to an extent which surprised him, revolved round the home, and what held the home together was the permanence of marriage.

The force of conventional morality certainly held nearly all marriages together; how much it contributed to the happiness of a good many is another question. By investing all matters of sexual behaviour, even the most innocent, with a cloak of secrecy and sinfulness, it did not make for understanding between men and women, nor even for easy social relationships, particularly when it was reinforced by boarding-school education. Of one school (Clayesmore) in 1899 *The Boy's Own Paper* approvingly remarked that there was no ladies' college within miles 'to tempt vain and budding youth to his doom'. Dog-keeping, on the other hand,

The marriage market, from an engraving after George du Maurier, 1883. 'Marriage is, as it will continue to be, the grand object in life to every young Englishwoman,' T. H. S. Escott, about 1880

BRITISH WORKMAN

GEORGE STEPHENSON

MODELLING CLAY ENGINES

STEPHENSON'S COTTAGE AT WILLINGTON.

STUDYING THE STEAM-ENGINE

THE WONDERFUL RAILWAY ENGINEER.

The wildest romance that was ever written, is not so marvellous as some true stories of the lives of great men. Out of the humblest homes, in the lowest depths of social life, God has sometimes caused a man to arise, who has attained to the summit of human greatness, and left his impress on the institutions of his age and country: like the lark, that builds its lowly nest amid the clods of the valley, and yet soars aloft, and sings its morning song above the clouds. But, of course, the instances are rare of such progress from the lowly to the lofty, and sometimes the cases are more wonderful

H. ANELAY.

J. JOHNSTON

was encouraged—'the value of a little practical knowledge on the subject of breeding is incalculable'.

If pleasure was sinful, that was mainly because it came between a man and his work, and the virtuousness of working hard was correspondingly exalted. Work lay at the centre of middle-class life. Without work a man could not rise; without work he could not hold his position; without work he might be ruined, and the terrors of falling into ruin, with very little in the way of a State safety-net underneath, were very much greater than they are today. The necessity and the virtue of work, therefore, had always been foremost in the middle-class creed: under Victoria they were unceasingly preached at the labouring poor, who needed a good deal of convincing that their kind of work could have any virtue about it at all, and at the upper classes, who were not easily persuaded that the work the middle classes had in mind was always so necessary and so virtuous as they made out. Sometimes it looked rather like money-grubbing.

Whatever may be thought of some aspects of middle-class moralizing, in this insistence on the duty of working hard there was no humbug; what they preached at other people they practised themselves. George Stephenson, at the height of his career, would be up at daybreak or before and would go on until well into the evening, riding, walking, inspecting, dictating (once, it is said, for twelve hours at a stretch, until his secretary almost fell off his seat with weariness), instructing his pupils ('you young fellows don't know what *wark* is'), trying to solve his problems as he lay in bed. His son Robert claimed to have walked between London and Birmingham fifteen times during the building of the London and Birmingham railway. I. K. Brunel almost certainly worked himself to death, making matters worse by combining immense industry with a lively appetite for social life and parties. Sir Daniel Gooch of the Great Western Railway, as a young man, drove a train from Paddington to Exeter and back in a day—387 miles—after being out early in the morning to make ready. He spent his time at Exeter on matters connected with the line and during the day he only sat down for an hour, at dinner-time.

These great railway engineers were heroic, pioneering figures and to that extent exceptional, but they were representative men—representative, that is, of the Victorian middle classes at the peak of their energy and achievement, and they probably drove themselves no harder than many of their obscure contemporaries. And as the men

183

at the top worked hard, so they expected hard work of those they employed. The hours worked by dressmakers and shop assistants are well known. It is less well known, perhaps, that clerks might also work a twelve-hour day. At a London soap works, for instance, clerks were long expected in the counting house by six a.m. and there they stayed till six in the evening. By 1878 life was getting softer and it was becoming difficult to get them in on time, so the starting hour was altered to seven a.m. and two clerks every day had to stay after six p.m. to get orders ready for the morning. It was not until 1894 that the clerks were allowed to go at 5.30 p.m. and then the dinner hour was cut in half to compensate.

These clerks worked for a partnership (John Knight & Sons) which was in the hands of members of the founder's family who managed the business as well as owning it. They employed 150 men or so in the mid-century and the firm was fairly large by the standards of the day. It worked mainly, as all other soap firms did, for a local market (Knights' was the London market), but it was large enough to have a national reputation and from time to time the Knight partners would meet their competitors over fourteen-course dinners, often at the Great Eastern Hotel, to discuss matters of common interest, especially competition, which for many years was held more or less successfully under control so that everybody got a decent living from the trade. 'Our competition and rivalry', said a soap maker in 1886, 'has become like a game at billiards or cricket.'

Upon private partnerships like this, with unlimited liability, running businesses of moderate size, Victorian middle-class prosperity was chiefly built. Some businesses were much larger, especially in shipbuilding and the iron and steel trades, or amongst the great brewers. There were innumerable smaller undertakings, right down to the single craftsman at work behind his tiny shop. But the great public company, with thousands of shareholders and professional management, was a rarity, except on the railways, until very late indeed in Victoria's reign, even though the principle of limited liability, given Parliamentary blessing by the Companies Act of 1862, had been increasingly widely acted upon. It was the absence of large companies, publicly owned, which made worthwhile middle-class salaried jobs so hard to find above the clerical level.

Private businesses provided comfort, even opulence, for their owners. Four Knight partners, in the later sixties, were sharing yearly profits ranging from £15,520 to £17,303, and at about the same time a soap firm in Bristol was producing profits up to nearly £19,000, though it is fair to add that in some years they fell to less than half that. On revenues like these the principal partners could live in some style and cut a figure, if they wished, in local affairs. It was from this class that mayors and aldermen came, whose statues adorn provincial squares and whose bequests and benefactions produced libraries, swimming baths, hospitals, churches and many other institutions which did something to relieve urban gracelessness.

In private firms of moderate size the family and business interests of the owners were not sharply distinguished. The Knights several times recorded gifts to poor relations in their minute books and their attitude to their staff had something of family life in it too. Their minutes fairly often record that some one was 'remonstrated with by the Firm', very rarely that anyone was dismissed. A foreman carter for many years periodically disgraced himself by getting drunk and staying away from work, once for as much as a week, but he was not sacked until he was on the verge of *delirium tremens* and even after that the firm eventually took him on again, though not as a foreman. A clerk once left of his own accord, and of him the Firm remarked: 'After many years service during the whole of which he had given more or less dissatisfaction to the Firm W. Thornton bade us good-bye today intending to set up in some small business on his own account—in which we hope he will do well.' Men past their work—sometimes their widows after them—were pensioned by the firm: ex-employees were sometimes buried at the firm's expense. At the beginning of each year, when wages and salaries were revised, gifts were regularly distributed, in spite of efforts to stop the practice, which ran between a few shillings and £10.

Paternalism took many forms. William Fairbairn of Manchester, in the forties, would instantly sack any man found drinking in his engineering works. 'I wish', he said, 'to have an orderly set of workmen; and in the next place I am decidedly of opinion that it is better for the men themselves and for their families.' He also disliked seeing any man of his untidy on a Sunday. 'I do not, perhaps, speak to him then,' he said, 'but on the Monday I tell him . . . that I find he has as good wages as other men who dress respectably, and that I do not like to have anyone about me who will not dress well on the Sunday. This intimation has generally had

the desired effect.' One of the most thorough-going paterna-
lists was Sir Titus Salt, and a description of Saltaire (see
Chapter V) written in 1876 illustrates the activities of a
benevolent employer and the attitude of mind which under-
lay them. 'Saltaire', wrote W. Cudford in *Round about
Bradford*, 'has . . . been likened to a commercial Utopia.
As a town—and especially as a manufacturing town—it is a
marvel of cleanliness, cheerfulness, and beauty. Its inhabitants should be, whether they are or not, a superior
and happy people. With constant work, decent homes, and
a munificent provision for instruction, amusement, and
recreation close at hand, we cannot imagine any rational
cause for discontent. Of course, ripe fruit does not drop into
one's mouth unplucked even at Saltaire. The "dignity of
labour" is upheld there in its integrity, and "charity", in
its demoralizing sense, is unrecognized either by the

Sir Titus Salt's new factory and workers' dwellings at Saltaire, from an engraving of c 1877. 'If the adage be true that the man who makes two blades of grass grow where but one grew before is a benefactor of his kind, what shall we say of the man who has created a manufacture of such magnitude as that with which Sir Titus Salt was connected?' (From *The Modern Portrait Gallery,* 2nd series)

employer or employed. The provision of so many dwellings is a simple commercial transaction between Sir Titus and his employés. For those living outside, who need morning and mid-day refreshment, a capital breakfast or dinner is provided for a surprisingly small sum—but everything must be paid for however reasonable the sum may be. The utmost freedom and liberty is thus secured to all who reside in or are in any way connected with the place. In only one respect that we know of is there any restrictive veto exercised. Across the boundary line is written this inexorable edict— "All beer abandon ye that enter here." The consequence is that "fuddlers" find no abiding place at Saltaire.'

The writer of Murray's Handbook for Yorkshire of 1882 saw less evidence of 'freedom and liberty' in the conception of Saltaire and called it 'very Russian—the work of one autocratic mind'. Certainly much of what Salt and Fairbairn did, and many others of like mind, was an intrusion into people's private lives and an attempt to enforce middle-class ideas of conduct where there was no reason to suppose they would be welcome. But in an authoritarian age, when people were accustomed to judge all matters of conduct by what they held to be absolute standards of morality, there were few to question an employer's right to regulate his men's private behaviour if he wished, particularly if he looked after them well in other ways.

Paternalism, in the heyday of the Victorian middle classes, was the mark of a good employer, and generally of one in a way of business sufficiently large to free him from petty worries which might make a smaller man mean. He could afford, perhaps, to send his workmen and their families—a thousand people—in two special trains on a free trip to the seaside for a day, as Gossages of Widnes did in 1879. And if he did not take care of his people, when there was little in the way of State welfare services, it was pretty certain that no one else would.

By the time benevolence on Gossages' scale became possible some of life's harshness, for the middle class as for the working class, was beginning to soften. Families were moving into the second or third generation of prosperity; they had 'arrived' and were getting used to it. Their manner of life was beginning to pass from the strictness of the days of struggle towards much wider, not to say looser, views.

The first major sign that the middle classes were turning their attention seriously—and the word is used advisedly— to matters of amusement was the emergence of organized team games from, say, the sixties onwards. 'Sport', formerly, to the aristocratic mind, had been mainly a matter of horses, hounds, guns, prize-fighters, or any form of contest, including cricket, which bets could be laid on. For the populace in general it had usually been some form of fight, including football, and part of its attraction had often been cruelty to animals, as in bearbaiting, though in fairness it must be admitted that boxers, single-stick fighters, wrestlers, footballers and others were almost as ready to exchange cruelty amongst themselves as to inflict it on bulls, dogs and fighting cocks. What is very certain is, first, that no one saw anything morally elevating in 'sport' and, second, that little in the nature of 'team spirit' existed, except when one village turned out to scrag another in some unregulated form of football or when two sets of professional or semi-professional cricketers were set at each other so that gentlemen could gamble on the result. 'Sport', to put the matter briefly, represented a great many aspects of the old, unruly, unregenerate England which the middle-class mind deplored.

But 'manliness' it undoubtedly encouraged, and that was a quality which the middle classes prized. Moreover, it was competitive, and competition was one of the great driving forces in middle-class life. Therefore if sport could be brought under some kind of civilized control, purged of its grosser cruelties and separated from the gambling instinct, it might at one and the same time provide an outlet for physical energy and be made to teach improving moral lessons: a highly desirable combination of functions. And team games, besides providing amusement for greater numbers than the older individualistic forms of sport, had moralities of their own which schoolmasters, especially, were quick to seize upon. They were certainly a great improvement on the older boarding-school pastimes of fighting, bullying, drinking, wenching and periodic rebellion.

By the time Lord Clarendon's Commission investigated the great public schools in the early sixties, games in something like their modern form were already firmly established, although it was not until some time later that they locked the public-school mind in an all-embracing grip, becoming identified, as they did so, both with the virtues of Christianity and the qualities demanded by late-Victorian imperial enthusiasm. As 'character training' steadily overhauled the training of the mind as the prime aim of English education, so 'games' came to stand for nearly everything that was worth having in the masculine nature (and even girls'

A cycling match between H. P. Whiting and Hon Keith Falconer, 1875

188

Cricket: Oxford v Cambridge. Painting by R. Davidson, 1859.
'If ever the University match should cease to be played, a great blow
will be struck at amateur cricket, for these matches are a model of
what all matches ought to be.' Hon R. H. Lyttleton, 1888. The first
University match was played in 1827, and it became an annual
event in 1838

191

schools were infected with the fever too). Intellectual attainments became highly suspect, as presumptive evidence of unmanly character and almost a disgrace in themselves. It was not altogether a healthy situation for a country which was beginning to need all the brains it could find to hold its commercial place in the world.

Outside the schools, the spread of organized games did something to tame the barbarity of popular amusements. At Wednesbury soccer started in 1873, cycling and cricket two years later. In the slums of London, during the eighties and later, earnest and muscular young men from the public schools and the universities began to make some impression, with team games and boxing, on the wild children of the back streets. Saturday football, from the seventies on, began to emerge as one of the main amusements of the working man, and a comparatively harmless one, but what the early enthusiasts did not foresee, and certainly did not intend, was that it would become increasingly a spectacle presented by professional players for the benefit of a non-playing audience.

In middle-class suburban life itself, from the sixties onwards, sports clubs of all kinds were founded—for 'Scotch golf', for Rugby football, for lawn tennis (an invention of the seventies) and, above all, for cricket, which by the seventies had emerged from its rather shady past to become the embodiment of all the qualities, moral as well as physical, which the Englishman thought he developed from games-playing—an improbable achievement, really, for a game so remarkably unsuited to the English climate. In games, as in other departments of life, class distinction began to show; rugger and cricket, broadly speaking, were games for gentlemen, soccer for the working classes. In rather the same category as games, for the middle classes, came service in the Volunteers, which from 1859 onwards combined physical exercise and pleasant company with a satisfying feeling of doing one's patriotic duty. Professional military opinion rated the Volunteers rather low, but that did nothing to check enthusiasm, and by 1863 there were enough volunteers for 20,000 of them to take part in a field day (Monday, 6th April) at Brighton. *The Times* recorded some of the proceedings: 'The Middlesex Artillery guns were horsed from Pickford's stud, great care being taken in matching colours, and in supplying the drivers with uniform jackets and regulation short whips. The Sussex and Cinque Ports Artillery, on the contrary, had their guns drawn by horses of all

192

Instructing the Volunteers: engraving after John Leech, c 1860. Since Volunteer Regiments were private clubs, and their members not usually poor men, they could allow themselves considerable whimsicality in the uniforms they provided themselves with. As the contrast between the regular Sergeant and the Volunteers shows, they did not necessarily follow the regular pattern and were apt to show some Continental influence

colours, and attended by carters in their rough smock-frocks, with the long-handled whips of agricultural labour. . . . The country carters, many of them wearing rosettes in honour of the occasion, made their horses travel past at a speed which the Middlesex Artillery did not attempt. . . . The animals became as excited as the men, or else seemed lost in wonder at the novelty of the event, and one huge "wheeler" placed between the shafts of a gun carriage, resigning himself to circumstances with a very bad grace, was dragged along the turf by his companions very much in the posture of a sitting elephant.' The ardour of the sixties was no mere passing craze, and by the mid-nineties there were over 200,000 Volunteers. All in all, it is easy to believe the young man who assured Taine that he knew nothing of 'young men leading irregular lives', because 'a man is kept very busy in London by the duties of his profession, by his family, by sport, cricket, riding and service in the Volunteers'.

Towards the end of the century, one can picture the well-to-do Victorian middle-class family in its solid suburban house, with a semi-circular carriage drive running from the

Croquet and crinolines in the 1880s, at Jayes Park, Ockley, Surrey. The Dowager Lady Abinger is on the right

gate past the shrubbery up to the front door and out again on the other side. The carriage drive was likely to symbolize aspiration rather than fact, unless the family was really wealthy, for it needed a great deal of money to run a carriage, and most middle-class families had to wait for the motor car before they could have their own private transport. But at least there would be ample money to staff the house, to take the whole family to the seaside every year (with appropriate servants), or perhaps abroad, to educate the boys and launch them into professional life, and to provide for the girls adequately.

In the family's general way of life, it was likely that there would be little enough of puritan austerity. Drink might still be suspect, but on the other hand there might be an excellent cellar of wines. The head of the family, whose father might have gone to work at nine in the morning and stayed till nine at night, would be likely now to leave at five; work was not quite the all-consuming necessity it once had been. For amusement, it was unlikely that theatres or dancing would be barred. Certainly relations between the sexes would be somewhat easier than thirty or forty years before, partly

because new amusements—croquet, lawn tennis, roller-skating, cycling—had brought young men and young women much more informally into each other's presence.

Of behaviour at skating rinks, Escott observed 'in plain words it signified the revolt of the sons and daughters of the middle class against their exclusion from modes of social enjoyment that to their contemporaries slightly above them in the social scale had long been allowed'. By the seventies, that is to say, the force of the middle-class attack on the privileged position of the upper classes had carried them well within it. They had impressed their own notions on many aspects of upper-class life; in return, they were allowing upper-class notions to modify some of their own. In the process, some of the grimness of middle-class life rubbed off; some of the wilder excesses of aristocratic self-indulgence were tamed. A kind of life emerged which, if it had a good deal of snobbery, purse-pride and smugness about it, was nevertheless a good deal more humane and civilized than either aristocratic or middle-class life in the not very distant past.

9 The passing of an age

An early motor-car, produced by the City and
Suburban Carriage Co of London: the rear-driven
Electric Victoria (the Queen had one) of 1901. It
seated two inside, with a coachman behind. Its range
on one charge was 35–40 miles at 12 mph. Upholstered
in the best coach cloth, with a folding hood, it had
three-inch pneumatic tyres, silver-plated electric
lamps, bells and fittings, and patent leather wings
and front dash. Complete with set of tools, the price
was £570.

The Queen in 1890

The last survivor of Sir John Moore's army at Corunna lived until 1889. Gladstone, born in 1809, died in 1898. The Queen herself lived from 1819 to 1901. Here were three people, like others who lived as long, who saw England virtually out of the eighteenth century into the beginning of the twentieth, and no doubt it is the fact that the Victorian period, by definition, covered no more than one long lifetime that gives it its underlying unity. For the Queen's reign, by conventional reckoning, covered two generations, and they differed as well as resembled each other. The first Victorians created the material framework of a whole new way of life; their works were monumental, their lives austere. The second generation built on their fathers' work. They had less need to be giants; they lived in easier times. The locomotive they did not invent; the bicycle they did. It was symbolic of many changes that were coming over English life in Queen Victoria's later years.

For the first time, private transport was cheap—cheap enough even for the working man. Bicycles built by village blacksmiths in the seventies cannot have saved much effort —they were much too heavy for that—but they did cut distance and save time. They carried labourers to work and country postmen on their rounds. Further up the social scale the bicycle was for play rather than work, but its effects were not less far-reaching for that. 'There are bicycling clubs', says Escott, 'in every part of England, which have their periodic meetings. A favourite rendez-vous in the neighbourhood of London is Bushey Park, and there, when the weather is fine, as many as a thousand bicyclists congregate. During the summer, too, in the heart of the city, when the business traffic of the day is done and the streets are clear, an active scene may often be witnessed by gaslight. Under the shadow of the Bank and the Exchange, the asphalte thoroughfare is covered with a host of bicycle riders, performing a series of intricate evolutions on their iron steeds.'

With the bicycle, the roads began to revive after their long eclipse by the railway train, and battered enamel notices put up by the Cyclists Touring Club ('Caution: this hill is dangerous' and the like) still remain to remind the twentieth century of the late nineteenth. The townsman began to see something of the country; the countryman was brought closer to the town. Women soon took to bicycles and they helped to remove some of the starch from men's and women's behaviour towards each other. The bicycle was an emancipator and a broadener, and one not confined, as liberating influences so often had been in the past, to the upper classes. Indeed, it is probably reasonable to guess that the people who got most from it were the youth of the lower end of the middle classes—clerks and small business men—of the generation of Lupin Pooter and his friends.

Even more important as a form of cheap private transport, though in Victorian times and for many years later much more restricted in its social range, was the motor car. Large, fast cars were for wealthy sportsmen and were in general the embodiment of rich and arrogant privilege, but not the small low-powered cars of one or two cylinders, selling for somewhere between £100 and £200. And they were already fairly common before Queen Victoria died. A letter in *The Autocar* of 1901 speaks of 'the large number of reliable cars about, capable of doing their twenty miles

Tricycling *à la mode*, 1889

an hour, and very few involuntary stops'. A small car could be run for about 4d. (about 1½p) a mile, whereas even the cost of so humble a horse-drawn vehicle as a pony-trap (unless you were a farmer) might run to 6d. (2½p) a mile, and this is a figure for a doctor in a country practice. Anything more pretentious, especially in town, would be so much more costly as to be out of reach of most middle-class families, even those comfortably off. Many town doctors, before small cars, did their rounds on foot and on public transport. The force of the term 'carriage folk' is shown by the very few Victorian suburban houses, even the most substantial, which had any provision, in the form of stabling or coach-houses, for any form of private transport at all.

The cheapening of private transport in the second half of Victoria's reign was a revolution as far-reaching as the cheapening of public transport by railways in the first half. Its full effects lie a long way beyond the death of Victoria and, indeed, are only now beginning to become apparent, with the motor car taking the place of the bicycle as Every-man's transport. But before the Queen died the motor car was a commercial proposition and the bicycle was an established part of the national life.

In another field of communication—the passing of messages rather than the transport of goods and people—the early Victorians developed the penny post, itself made possible by railways, and the electric telegraph. The late Victorians, in the last twenty years or so of the Queen's life, added the telephone and the typewriter. The strictly economic effects of these two inventions in the speeding-up of business are not here our direct concern. In the social life of the country, which is our concern, there were perhaps no other inventions which did more to make jobs for women outside the home.

The telegraph service employed women from the start. There were two, according to the Census Report, as early as 1851 (out of 284 people altogether), and the figure rose a great deal in the sixties. With the development of telephone exchanges it shot ahead. Men were employed at first, but it soon became apparent that this was a job which women did, if anything, rather better, and by the end of the century over forty per cent of the people in the telegraph and telephone service were women.

The typewriter had even more startling results. Before the eighties the idea of a woman employed in an office was practically unheard of. The number of women clerks re-

200

turned at the 1881 Census was negligible. By 1891 nearly 18,000 were returned; by 1901, 55,784—seven per cent of all business and commercial clerks. The Census Report comments 'there is an increasing tendency to the employment of female clerks . . . Very probably many . . . were typewriters.'

Poor girls, as previous chapters have shown, had long gone out to work as a matter of necessity, but the kind of work they could get was not such as to attract anyone whom necessity did not drive pretty hard. Slightly higher in the social scale, where the force of circumstances was only a little less pressing, the possibilities were very limited. Teaching was a predominantly female occupation, but apart from that (which might be held to include governessing) there was little. Dressmaking and shop-assisting both had deservedly bad reputations for overwork and general tyranny. Nursing, greatly improved since the forties when Southwood Smith had remarked 'the generality of nurses in hospitals are not such as the medical men can place much confidence in', only employed about fifty-one women in ten thousand. There was really very little for the girl who was above 'service' or factory work, and most of what there was had serious disadvantages. Moreover, it was pretty generally considered unladylike for a woman to go out to work at all and, if she did, the assumption was that her family could not support her. Jobs as telephonists and 'typewriters'

A telephone exchange, from an engraving of 1883. A telephone exchange opened in Lombard Street, London, in 1879. 'Mr Edison', wrote Arnold White, Secretary and Manager of the Edison Telephone Company of London (Limited) on 20th August 1879, 'has lately given the subject of Telephone Exchanges his earnest attention, and has devised means, at once efficient and simple, which supersede the noisy and expensive systems prevailing in the central bureaux in the United States. It is true that . . . the English commercial public are at present behind the age in respect to telephonic communication; but the Edison exchanges now being organized by this company will surpass in cheapness and efficiency anything of the kind known in America.' (*The Times*, 21st August 1879)

A typing pool, from an engraving
after J. H. Bacon, 1888

added to the range of women's opportunities. More important, they were the first cautious opening of a door into
what had hitherto been entirely a man's world. More important again, perhaps, they represented the first small chip
off the immense weight of prejudice against the idea of
women taking work outside the home, and they fore-
shadowed the time when taking a job would be a perfectly
normal thing for any girl to do, rather than a measure of
desperate need.

Higher in the social and educational scale, and connected
with the effort to improve women's education discussed in
Chapter 7, there arose a demand for women to be allowed
into the professions. 'They are . . . excluded wholly or in
great part from the Church, the law, and medicine,' said the
Census Report of 1871. 'Whether they should be rigidly
excluded from these professions, or be allowed—on the

principle of freedom of trade—to compete with men, is one of the questions of the day.' The women's assault was mainly directed against the masculine monopoly of medicine. In 1874 the London School of Medicine for Women was opened and two years later, after bitter controversy, an Act of Parliament allowed properly qualified women to be registered. By 1901, according to the Census, there were 335 'lady doctors'. They were still, to most people, highly suspect curiosities and they long remained so, but at least the right of women to enter a profession had been established, however grudgingly, and the highly educated girl of the class which traditionally expected a lady to remain unoccupied except by good works and marriage had at last some prospect of independence.

As long as there was no way of limiting the number of children a normally fertile couple could produce, a married woman's liberty was very severely curtailed unless her husband was at least comfortably off. Then she could have

A Lady Doctor, from an engraving of 1865. Elizabeth Blackwell (1821–1910) was placed on the Medical Register in 1858, with an American degree, and Elizabeth Garrett (1836–1917) in 1865, with the Licence of the Society of Apothecaries. After that the profession successfully blocked the qualification of women until Russell Gurney's 'Act to remove the Restrictions on the Granting of Qualifications on the Ground of Sex' was passed in 1876. 'Certain *persons*,' said *The Lancet* in 17th June 1882, 'have succeeded in passing the examinations thrown open to them, and others may do the same, but the common sense of the world and the good sense of the sex will no more permanently tolerate the unseemly invasion of an unsuitable province of labour than women, as a class, will ultimately show themselves fitted for the discharge of the duties they have rashly, and, as we believe, indecorously, undertaken.'

QUICK & SAFE
HUDSON'S SOAP
40
FORGET ME NOT
HUDSON'S
LEAVES
NO SMELL.

Soap was one of the first commodities marketed by modern methods of nation-wide brand advertising. The pioneer was W. H. Lever, later Lord Leverhulme, who advertised *Sunlight Soap* widely and with enormous success from 1885 onward. Within about ten years he had what was probably the largest soapworks in the world, at Port Sunlight in Cheshire (see illustration p. 131). This advertisement is by one of Lever's competitors, R. S. Hudson & Co of Liverpool, which was taken over by Lever Brothers Limited in 1908

help in looking after her children and her own time and energies would not be severely strained. From the lower end of the middle classes downwards she was likely to be very hard-worked indeed especially as, with better conditions of life, more and more babies grew up. For the really poor the arrival of yet another baby was nothing but a disaster. But by 1872 birth control was sufficiently practicable and respectable to be discussed openly in the *Fortnightly Review* —a periodical of somewhat advanced tendencies—and it was from about that time that it was practised more and more widely among the educated classes, as population statistics increasingly show. Among the working classes and the poor, whose need was greatest, it took much longer to arrive.

As, after 1870, more and more people learnt to read, new ideas of all kinds spread much more rapidly and the modern industry of mass communications began to take shape. The marketing of branded goods by large-scale advertising went ahead fast, provided with national coverage, from the mid-nineties on, by a new kind of popular press, brought into being very largely by Alfred Harmsworth, whose conception of popular journalism—*Answers* and the *Daily Mail* (1896)—was something that England had never seen before. Although Harmsworth's motives were at least partly political—he had a consuming urge for power—what he created did not in fact become part of the structure of politics like the old 'serious' newspapers and periodicals. He created a blend of entertainment and education, because his readers paid to be entertained but they could hardly avoid being educated, however painlessly, in the process. The kind of press which he created, like the cinema and television after it, was furiously assailed for sensationalism, distortion and debasement of taste. What was less often observed was that it catered for a genuine, if unsophisticated, curiosity about the world at large and, in so far as the British nation today may be said to be fit for self-government, the 'cheap' newspapers (as their detractors called them) ought to be allowed some of the credit for making it so.

National marketing and a national press were possible because late-Victorian England had been pulled together by the railways, the penny post, and the rest of the newly constructed apparatus of fast, cheap communication. From a collection of regions, separated rather than united by such means of transport as existed, England was becoming unified in a way never possible before. Enterprising business men

were quick to take the point; enterprising politicans also, and the ancient local basis of trade, politics and social life received a heavy blow.

From what has been said so far it will be evident that many influences which were to be important in English life long after the Queen's death had their beginnings in the seventies or thereabouts, when the first generation of Victorians was giving place to the second. To try to be exact in defining historical periods is to invite contradiction, but the seventies have a good claim on other than purely arithmetical grounds to be regarded as the dividing line between 'early' and 'late' Victorian England. It may be said with a good

Forsyte England, from an engraving after George du Maurier, 1878. 'It is the footman's duty to carry messages or letters for his master or mistress to their friends, to the post, or to the tradespeople; and nothing is more important than despatch and exactness in doing so.' *Mrs Beeton's Book of Household Management*, 1895 edition

deal of truth, for example, that in two ministries—Gladstone's from 1868 to 1874 and Disraeli's from 1874 to 1880—Victorian parliamentary politics reached their zenith. Certainly under these ministries, of both parties, the hopes of many early-Victorian reformers became the law of the land. Looking forward, they were the first ministries in England elected on anything like a democratic suffrage, thus foreshadowing the politics of the twentieth century.

In the same volume of the *Fortnightly* as the article on birth control there was an article by Francis Galton called 'A Statistical Enquiry into the Efficacy of Prayer'. Its conclusions were sceptical. It seems unlikely that such an expression of religious doubt could have been published in so respectable, if radical, a periodical much earlier in Victoria's reign. It seems equally unlikely that doubt of this kind began to assail many minds among the mass of ordinary Christians until much later. Nevertheless, when the article was published, *The Origin of Species* had been out for thirteen years, German textual criticism was eroding belief in the literal truth of the Bible, and in general the assault on traditional Christianity was well under way among the intellectuals. Tennyson, perhaps the poet who, among all others, most Victorians would have called their own, was affected by it by the time he published *In Memoriam*—1850. *In Memoriam* is a metrical essay on doubt. '. . . Time, a maniac scattering dust, And Life, a Fury slinging flame'—these lines, and many others, are not an expression of orthodoxy, nor were they meant to be.

Doubt of all kinds gathered force as time went on. The very prosperity of the late Victorians was not to the liking of all of them; not, at any rate, in all its forms. Trollope, in *The Way We Live Now*, castigated what he considered to be the corruption of society, especially the old rural society, by town-based 'financiers' symbolized by the unlikely figure of Melmotte. Thomas Hughes, preaching in Clifton College Chapel in 1879, attacked the materialism of the age and said: 'The standard of expenditure has been increasing by leaps and bounds, and demoralizing trade, society, every industry, and every profession, until a false ideal has established itself, and the aim of life is too commonly to get, not to be, while men are valued more and more for what they have, not for what they are.' This was a kind of sentiment which Matthew Arnold, William Morris and many others expressed in one way or another and which impelled some middle-class intellectuals to move towards the left of politics, with

207

important results for the leadership of the parties of protest in the nineties and much later.

The prosperity of England was not only threatened by the consciences of intellectuals. The sixties were a decade of war, opening, in Europe, with the various campaigns of the Italian *Risorgimento* and closing with the Prussian victory over France in 1871. Across the Atlantic, the Americans fought each other, between 1861 and 1865, in the first of the great modern wars, with more than a million men engaged on either side. The effect of these wars, at first, was entirely favourable to England, inasmuch as they stopped industrial rivals from developing as fast as they should have done. But in the seventies, with America recovering and expanding very fast and with Germany united under Prussia, the threat to England's industrial supremacy grew and grew.

As long as Germany was a loose or loosish federation of small states, German competition was not very serious, and indeed many ambitious young Germans came to England to better themselves, so that there was a continual complaint that German clerks were filching jobs that ought to have gone to Englishmen. But even while matters stood thus, there was an uneasy feeling in England that German technical education was better than anything England could show. Hence the commissions of enquiry into English schools, during the sixties, which have been referred to frequently in earlier chapters. Their most important recommendations unfortunately were passed over, and England had no comprehensively organized system of secondary education until the twentieth century. The flourishing public schools were not an adequate substitute in the matter of technical education, because their bias was still heavily towards the classics and literary studies generally, and because, in general, they did not care to concern themselves very closely with the class of boy who was likely to make his living in industry.

Nevertheless the growing threat from Germany and America could not be ignored, and a certain amount was done for secondary and higher education outside the range of the public schools and the ancient universities. By the nineties a good many of the old grammar schools had been set on their feet again by schemes of reorganization under the Endowed Schools Acts of 1869 and 1874. The School Boards, in a good many places, set up 'higher grade elementary schools' where history, grammar, French, mathematics and the elements of the physical sciences were taught. But

A board-school visitor, from an engraving after Charles Keene, 1882. 'But, it will be said, the child of today has the inestimable advantage of Education. No: he has not. Educated the children are not. They are pressed through "standards" which exact a certain acquaintance with ABC and pothooks and figures, but educated they are not in the sense of the development of their latent capacities so as to make them capable for the discharge of their duties in life.' 'General' Booth, of the Salvation Army, *In Darkest England*, 1890

this kind of teaching could not be supported by government grant. It had to be paid for either by fees or by grants from the Science and Art Department, which by 1894 was distributing about £143,000 a year and encouraging a heavy bias towards science in the schools which it supported. With these unsatisfactory methods of finance combined with the fact that pupils had to leave at fourteen, the 'higher grade elementary schools' were not altogether well fitted to provide the kind of basic technical education which the country increasingly needed. In any case, in 1895 there were only sixty higher grade board schools outside London, and thirty-five were in Durham, Lancaster and York. Twenty-three counties had none.

Above the secondary level of education, there was a growing number of university colleges. They were founded

at various times from the foundation of University College, London, in 1828, onward, but particularly towards the latter end of the century, and like the proprietary schools they reflect various groups' views of what was wrong with the existing educational system. Thus University College, London, was founded to provide university education without religious teaching and without religious discrimination. Other colleges, such as Owens College, Manchester (1845), Mason University College, Birmingham (1875) and other foundations also showed a desire to escape from the domination of education by religion. Others were the product of the movement for higher education for women, such as Girton

(1869), Newnham (1871), Somerville (1879) and the Royal Holloway College (1886). Many, especially those founded in the seventies and later, were intended principally as technical colleges, and the founder of at least one (Sir Josiah Mason) directly expressed a wish 'to give all classes in Birmingham, in Kidderminster, and in the district generally, the means of carrying on their scientific studies as completely and thoroughly as . . . in the great science schools of the Continent'. There could be no plainer expression of the acute and justified anxiety which many people felt about competition from countries which, besides having greater natural resources than England, were also doing more to train their managers and workpeople. But there seems to have been a certain complacency about the late-Victorian mind which made it pretty well satisfied with things as they were and disinclined for radical change in the English way of doing things.

The threat from the Continent was not simply economic. It was military as well. English confidence was upset by the bellicose gestures of Napoleon III about 1859. The volunteers were revived, the coasts were fortified, and interest in military affairs, which had almost disappeared for forty years after 1815, began to grow. It had already been quickened by the Crimean War and the Indian Mutiny in the fifties. In the sixties, after the passing of the French scare, it was kept alive by the wars on the Continent and in America, and it was powerfully reinforced by the result of the Franco-Prussian War. From about 1870 onwards a military spirit developed in England which would have astonished Victorians of the first generation, mindful of the reaction after Waterloo. Some real anxiety arose about the possibility of foreign invasion. Chesney's *Battle of Dorking* (1871) is one of the best known of many books published during the forty-odd years before 1914 which attempt to imagine the course and consequences of an invasion that succeeds.

Military excitement was not unwelcome. The late Victorians, long at peace, began to fancy they desired the stimulus of war. They could easily idealize the military character because so many military virtues were comprehended by the quality of 'manliness' which they greatly admired. The nasty side of the whole business was something they had never seen and, in spite of William Howard Russell, scarcely heard of. Colonial campaigns of the kind in which Sir Winston Churchill had his early military experience looked like a superior kind of blood sport, with enough danger to give spice and not enough to be depressing, and our side always won in the end. 'What examples are to be found in the tales here retold,' wrote W. H. Fitchett in the preface to the twelfth edition of his *Deeds that Won the Empire*, 'not merely of heroic fortitude; of loyalty to duty stronger than the love of life; of the temper which dreads dishonour more than it fears death; of the patriotism which makes love of the Fatherland a passion.' Or, as H. S. Alford and W. D. Sword put it, in describing the loss and recovery of the Sudan: 'The love of victory and conquest is still strong within us, and the lust for war by the great nations of the world at the present time is only curbed by the fear of the dreadful and lasting consequences that might follow a defeat.'

The mood expressed by these words, published in 1898, was something more than the old bulldog patriotism which had inspired Englishmen for generations. It came pretty close to looking for a fight, and in much late-Victorian thought and writing it was linked with notions of racial superiority which were later to be associated with Fascism. It was not a peculiarly English mood. Other prosperous nations of the West, especially the Great Powers, were afflicted with the same dangerous exaltation. Passions were working up towards the European mass suicide of 1914.

The Canadians issued a stamp in 1898 which showed a map of the world with British possessions marked in red upon it. It carried the words: 'We hold a vaster Empire than has been.' This Empire and the spirit which sustained and enlarged it was very much a late Victorian creation: indeed, almost post-Victorian. When the men of the nineties and the early 1900s saw all that red on the map, when they looked at the power, wealth and well-being which England seemed to draw from it, their self-confidence was restored. The foundations laid by their fathers, it seemed, were strong enough to carry an imposing superstructure. If, here and there, it was unsound, if it was, perhaps, a little rigid, a little out-of-date, those were matters of comparatively minor importance which they themselves or future generations would no doubt put right. In the meantime they could take pride in a certain air of antiquarian eccentricity which added to their reputation in foreign eyes. For the confidence which the late Victorians felt in themselves was reflected in the attitude of the world at large. Other nations did not like England, as they showed when the Boer War broke out, but the magnitude of her achievement they were forced to admire. By the

212

end of the Queen's reign England, proud, powerful and imperial, had made such an impression on the minds of men that everywhere, even in republican America, the last sixty years of the nineteenth century have come to be known as the Victorian Age. Queen Victoria, like the Emperor Augustus, has given her name to one of the most famous and fortunate periods in world history.

'We hold a vaster Empire than has been'. Canadian stamp of 1898

Books on Victorian England

A small, personal selection from the vast literature generated during and since the period. Most of the Victorian books listed are fairly easy to obtain. Some have appeared in recent editions or reprints, and none should be beyond the resources of the public library service.

Recent Works on Victorian History and Biography

Most of these books contain bibliographies, some very extensive.

Banks, J. A., *Prosperity and Parenthood*, a Study of Family Planning among the Victorian Middle Classes, 1954

Bax, B. Anthony, *The English Parsonage*, 1964

Blake, Robert, *Disraeli*, 1966

Briggs, Asa, *The Age of Improvement*, 1959
Victorian Cities, 1963

Burn, W. L., *The Age of Equipoise (1852–1867)*, 1964

Checkland, S. G., *The Rise of Industrial Society in England, 1815–1885*, 1964

Clark, G. Kitson, *The Making of Victorian England*, 1966

Cole, G. D. H., and Postgate, Raymond, *The Common People 1746–1946*, 1949

Coleman, D. C., *Courtaulds,* Vol I *The Nineteenth Century, Silk and Crepe*, 1969

Ensor, R. C. K., *England 1870–1914*, 1936

Ferriday, Peter (Ed), *Victorian Architecture*, 1963

Girouard, Mark, *The Victorian Country House*, 1971

Hudson, Derek, *Munby, Man of Two Worlds*, 1972

Hughes, M. Vivian, *A London Family 1870–1900*, 1946

Inglis, K. S., *Churches and the Working Classes in Victorian England*, 1963

Jackson, J. A., *The Irish in Britain*, 1964

Lipman, V. D., *Social History of the Jews in England 1850–1950*, 1954

Magnus, Philip, *Gladstone: a Biography*, 1954

Manton, Jo, *Elizabeth Garrett Anderson*, 1965

Mathias, Peter, *The First Industrial Nation, an Economic History of Britain 1700–1914*, 1969

Newsome, David, *Godliness and Good Learning*, 1961

Perkin, Harold, *The Origins of Modern English Society 1780–1880*, 1969
The Age of the Railway, 1970

Reader, W. J., *Professional Men, the Rise of the Professional Classes in Nineteenth-Century England*, 1966

Rolt, L. T. C., *Isambard Kingdom Brunel*, 1957
George and Robert Stephenson, 1960

Thompson, Flora, *Lark Rise to Candleford*, 1945

Thompson, F. M. L., *English Landed Society in the Nineteenth Century*, 1963

Ward, W. R., *Victorian Oxford*, 1965

Wells, H. G., *An Experiment in Autobiography,* Vol I, 1934

Woodham-Smith, Cecil, *The Reason Why,* 1953
Queen Victoria, Her Life and Times, Vol I 1819–61, 1972

Woodruff, Philip, *The Men who ruled India*, 2 vols, 1954

Woodward, Llewellyn, *The Age of Reform 1815–1870*, 1962

Young, G. M. (Ed.), *Early Victorian England 1830–1865*, 2 vols, 1934
Victorian England, Portrait of an Age, 1936

Picture Books

Bott, Alan, *Our Fathers (1870–1900)*, 1931
   and Clephane, Irene, *Our Mothers*, 1932
Clive, Mary, *The Day of Reckoning*, 1964
Gernsheim, Helmut and Alison, *Roger Fenton, Photographer of the Crimean War*, His Photographs and his Letters from the Crimea, 1954
Lister, Raymond, *Victorian Narrative Paintings*, 1966
National Army Museum, *The Army in India, a photographic record 1850–1914*, 1968
Spiller, Brian, *Victorian Public Houses*, 1972
de Vries, Leonard, *Victorian Advertisements*, 1968
Winter, Gordon, *A Country Camera 1844–1914*, 1966
   Past Positive, London's Social History recorded in photographs, 1971

Victorian Works on Victorian England

There is a vast store of information on all kinds of subjects, from the discipline and studies of the University of Oxford to the white slave trade, in Victorian Parliamentary Papers. Nor do they make dull reading. Many Victorian officials had a direct and lively style of writing, and the volumes of evidence attached to many enquiries contain verbatim records of the speech of the time—from Headmasters of public schools to children employed in the Potteries—which cannot be found anywhere else.
A few of the more important and accessible papers:

Report . . . on an Enquiry into the Sanitary Condition of the Labouring Population, 1842
First Report of the Commissioners for inquiring into the State of Large Towns and Populous Districts, 1844
Report of the Cambridge University Commission, 1852
Report of the Oxford University Commission, 1852
First and Second Reports of the Children's Employment Commission, 1862
Report of the Public Schools Commission, 1864
Report of the Schools Enquiry Commission, 1868
Report of the Select Committee of the House of Lords on the working of the Contagious Diseases Act, 1868
Report . . . by the Examiners into Outrages near Manchester, 1868
Report of the Select Committee of the House of Lords on the Law relating to the Protection of young Girls, 1882
Report of the Royal Commission on the Housing of the Working Classes, 1885
Report by Mr Wilson Fox on the Wages and Earnings of Agricultural Labourers in the United Kingdom, 1900
Reports of the Censuses of 1841, 1851, 1861, 1871, 1881, 1891, 1901

There are contemporary descriptions of Victorian England, from various points of view and at various dates, in:
Booth, Charles E. (Ed), *Life and Labour of the People in London*, First Series, Poverty, 1902
   Second Series, Industry, 1903

216

Third Series, Religious Influences, 1902

    see also Albert Fried and Richard M. Elman, *Charles Booth's London*, containing select passages from the original work, 1969

Engels, F., *The Condition of the Working-Class in England in 1844*, with Preface written in 1892, 1892

Escott, T. H. S., *England, its People, Polity and Pursuits*, new and revised edn 1885

    Social Transformations of the Victorian Age, 1897

Johnston, William, *England as it is, Political, Social, and Industrial, in the middle of the Nineteenth Century*, 2 vols, 1851

Mayhew, Henry, *London Labour and the London Poor*, 1851

Taine, Hippolyte, *Notes on England* (ed. Edward Hyams), 1957

and there are diarists:

Armstrong, Revd B. J., *Armstrong's Norfolk Diary*, 1963

Evelyn, George Palmer, *A Diary of the Crimea*, 1954

Kilvert, Revd Francis, *Kilvert's Diary 1870–79*, ed William Plomer, 1964 (paperback)

Munby, A. J., *Munby, Man of two Worlds* by Derek Hudson, 1972

Romilly, Rev Joseph, *Romilly's Cambridge Diary 1832–42*, 1967

Russell, W. H., *My Diary in India in the year 1858–9*, new edn, n d

and for contemporary illustrations of the period see bound volumes of *Punch* and *Illustrated London News*.

Victorian Works on a variety of Subjects:

Arnold, Matthew, *Schools and Universities on the Continent*, 1868

    Culture and Anarchy, 1869

Butler, Samuel, *The Way of all Flesh*, 1903

Churchill, W. S., *The River War, the Reconquest of the Sudan*, 1899

    My Early Life, 1930

Doyle, Sir Arthur Conan, the Sherlock Holmes stories, various dates from 1887 onward

Eliot, George, *Middlemarch* and other novels

Galsworthy, John, *The Forsyte Saga*

Galton, Francis, *The Art of Travel*, 1860

Giffen, Sir Robert, *The Progress of the Working Classes in the last Half-Century*, 1884

Hodder, Edwin, *The Life of Samuel Morley*, 1887

Kipling, Rudyard, Select works, prose and verse

Mill, J. S., *The Subjection of Women*, 1869

Newbolt, Sir Henry, *Clifton Chapel*, 1909

Smiles, Samuel, *Self-Help*, 1859

    Lives of the Engineers, 5 vols, new edn 1874

Thomson, H. Byerley, *The Choice of a Profession*, 1857

Traill, H. D. (Ed), *Social England*, Vol VI, 1898

Trollope, Anthony, the Barchester novels; *The Way we Live Now*, 1875

Ward, Mrs Humphry, *Marcella*, 1894, and other Novels

Wolseley, F-M Viscount, *The Story of a Soldier's Life*, 1903

Index

The numerals in **heavy type** refer to pages on which illustrations appear

222

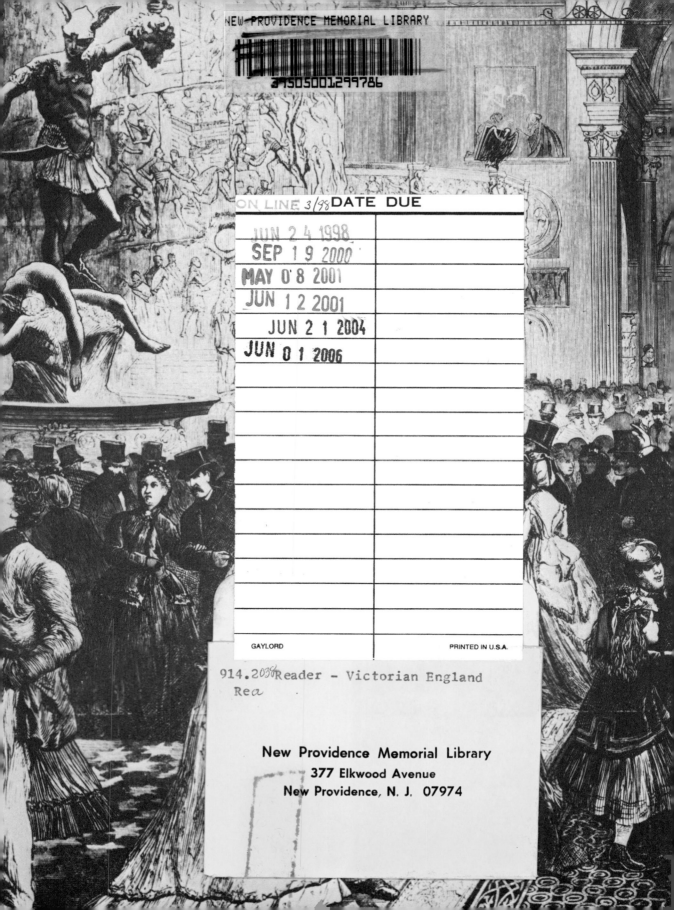